The Extraordinary Greek People

Their Remarkable Achievements and Philosophy for Living from Ancient Times to Today

MISSION POINT PRESS

Published by Mission Point Press
2554 Chandler Rd.
Traverse City, MI 49696
(231) 421-9513
www.MissionPointPress.com

Design by Sarah Meiers

ISBN 978-1-958363-36-2
Library of Congress Control Number 2022916753

Printed in the United States of America

The Extraordinary Greek People

*Their Remarkable Achievements
and Philosophy for Living
from Ancient Times to Today*

by Andrew E. Manatos

MISSION POINT PRESS

Dedication

I dedicate this book to my four grandparents Anna and Nicholas Manatos (Manatakis in Crete) and Kleanthe and Micheal Varanakis who as young people left their villages near Chania, in Apokoronas, Crete, Greece to come to the western United States during a very difficult era, particularly for foreigners. The unimaginable risks and hardships they lived through so that their children and their children's families could enjoy the best lives available to humankind, can never be appropriately thanked.

My grandparents' wisdom and the power of their example created 14 children and their spouses who for me were unsurpassed parents, uncles, and aunts. To a person, their welcome, wisdom, high standards of example, altruism, and love surrounded me like a safety net as they held my hand throughout their lives. And their wisdom and example created for me over 30 siblings, first cousins and their spouses who are also of unsurpassed high quality. Their sense of humor, wisdom, reliability, altruism, and love waiting in the wings are a constant comfort.

My grandparents provided their progeny with the tools and pattern of living, based on Hellenic values and Orthodoxy, that produce loving, fulfilling lives that few in the world can enjoy. They enabled each of us to thrive in our various circumstances as we played the somewhat different hand that life dealt to each of us. Life is mysterious and can pose significant difficulties but thank God for the example of our grandparents' huge sacrifices, we have been given the perseverance and perspective to enjoy fulfilling lives.

And, a special appreciation to my idyllic eight grandchildren, fantastic four sons, amazing three daughters-in-law, and wonderful wife who have surrounded me with humankind's warmest, softest possible familial cushion. I am blessed.

Table of Contents

INTRODUCTION

British Prime Minister Winston Churchill, one of the 20th century's most revered figures, said of the Greek people,

> *The passage of thousands of years sees no diminution in their original vitality ... an inheritance of wisdom and genius.*

This slim volume is an introduction to the vast Greek accomplishments many of which have managed to surpass all other civilizations or nationalities. It is also a look at the myriad contributions that have significantly improved the lives of the nearly eight billion people alive today. What follows could also be described as a retrospective of the astounding triumphs of the Greek people. In the cases that are fairly well known, we hope to present new information that puts these accomplishments into perspective, underscoring their importance. Hellenes and humanitarians may find themselves filled with emotion as they read touching stories of courage and sacrifice.

Some of this exploration will focus on the accomplishments of Hellenes in America, particularly in the Washington public policy area. It does describe the many successful and famous Greeks in America to which Wikipedia devotes 26 pages—https://en.wikipedia.org/wiki/List_of_Greek_Americans. A proper enumeration and description of these extraordinary people would require a book in and of itself. They range from television and movie stars like Jennifer Aniston (Anastasakis) to one of America's top space scientists for whom the International Astronomical Union named an asteroid—Stamatios Krimigis.

It spends a great deal of its focus on Hellenic traits. This is the case because America is one of the countries where the Greek culture of Hellenism can be examined and compared alongside virtually all other cultures of the world. Subtle positive Greek characteristics, possibly not even noticed by Hellenes, are brought into stark relief in this diverse nation.

Many people living in Greece have not been exposed to America's melting pot of cultures. And, therefore, some in Greece may take for granted positive aspects of their culture—and themselves—that are truly quite special. Some may assume that most people around the world live in a similar fashion. We'll point to important surveys and studies that highlight these positive and unique traits.

This book's descriptions of unique Greek personality traits may even cause some Hellenic readers to come away with a better understanding of themselves. It may have a similar effect had by our video about Greek *philotimo* (the love of honor) on an older Greek American with one Greek parent, who was not particularly involved in Hellenism and was no longer a part of the Greek Orthodox Church. After viewing this *philotimo* video, he wrote to us and said,

> *I came across your YouTube presentation on* Philotimo. *What an eye-opening explanation of what has been an overwhelming and basic part of my life. I never understood it, or where it came from, or why it is a driving force in my personality. Now more than ever I can see why I am the way I am. Thank you so very much, your impact on my life through this experience is greatly appreciated.*

The *philotimo* video, officially titled *The Greek Secret*, can be viewed at https://www.oxidayfoundation.org/philotimo/the-greek-secret/. In this document, you are reading 3,000 words spent describing and telling stories of touching *philotimo*.

This is not only a story of the past but also of the present. The culture, Hellenism, of the well-known Golden Age of Greece some 2,500 years ago was not a one-time event. It was passed on and instilled in subsequent generations of Greeks including today's. Greeks continue to take leaps forward for humankind. Over the roughly 90 generations since the Golden Age, the Greek people retained far more than traditional names, like Zoe and Penelope,

Athena and Alexander, Theodore and Telly (for Telemachus, son of the mythical Odysseus). They also retained the magic of Hellenism. It is remarkable that the accomplishments over the years of one nationality who make up only 1/645th of the world's population could achieve such a high percentage of the world's advancements.

Some Greeks in the United States may not fully appreciate their unique culture. This book is in many ways intended for them, but it is also meant to be of particular value for young people of Greek descent and for all young people, too—not just as a guide to the past, but also as a guide to the future.

It is very difficult for any young person to know which path to choose in education and career, love and family, and how one sees the world. Such choices are crucial, and a Hellenic life built on valuing the history of the Greek people, the steps to a "good life," a knowledge of Greek achievements, and ties to the Greek community where you live can help guide the way. Hopefully, this will reduce the number of Hellenes and others who casually discard traditional Hellenic pathways in their youth. It can save them from discovering later in life that they ignored something very special that can bring them happiness and fulfillment by helping others.

As we explain, Hellenism is an all-encompassing cultural environment. It can improve and strengthen many, if not all, aspects of one's life—Greek or non-Greek. Journalist and author Malcolm Gladwell expresses well the importance of our environment. He said,

> *The culture we belong to and the legacies passed down by our forebearers shape the patterns of our achievement in ways we cannot begin to imagine. It is only by asking a person where they are from that we can unravel the logic behind who succeeds. The tallest oak in the forest is not just the tallest because it grew from the heartiest acorn. It is also the tallest because no other trees blocked its sunlight, the soil around it was deep and rich, no rabbit chewed through its bark when it was a sapling, and because no lumberjack cut it down before it matured. We all know that successful people come from hearty seeds, but do we know enough about the sunlight that warmed them, the soil in which they*

put down their roots, and the rabbits and lumberjacks they
were lucky enough to avoid?

Here are just a few areas where Hellenism can improve one's life: bringing a new life into this world; devotion to progeny; herd protection of the young by immediate family, extended family and *koumbari* (explained later); the cushioning of surroundings and safety net from nonfamily but familial-Hellenes and *philotimo* (explained later); protections against ill health, alcoholism, dementia, and truncated lifespan; through millennial-old paths to success and "the good life"; the courage to question mob leadership and learn the benefits of sacrifice, work, and competition; and our faith of love, respect, humility, and dignity.

In America, and likely in other Greek diaspora communities, maintaining Hellenism is not always easy—certainly not as easy as just jettisoning one's heritage and luxuriating in popular culture. It may be more difficult in America than in Australia where, for example, Hellenes make up a higher percentage of the population, while Hellenes in America account for one out of every 250. Also, given the far more recent Greek emigration to Australia compared to the emigration of Greeks to America, the Greek Australians are roughly one generation closer to those who grew up in Greece. Even so, the preservation of Hellenism everywhere outside of Greece requires an extra effort and brings rich rewards.

This task of preserving Greek culture and pride in Hellenism is urgent. It can be seen in our churches which also serve as a center for Hellenism. A tabulation of baptisms in the Greek Orthodox Church in America suggests our numbers are diminishing as is the case in other churches. If Greek Orthodox Church baptisms diminish at the rate that they have fallen—from 9,200 baptisms in 1994 to 5,800 in 2014—our 500 churches in America will average only three baptisms annually by 2045. That can have a huge impact on Hellenism.

The Greek Orthodox Church is countering this decline in baptisms in America. Without sacrificing its truths, the church is renewing its connection to its flock with the appointment of an extraordinary and young Archbishop of America, Elpidophoros. He is doing everything possible to reverse this trend. He has been extremely well received by the Greek Orthodox community and especially among its youth and women. His leadership resolved for the church many multimillion-dollar financial hurdles it was facing.

Churchill's comments about Greek wisdom and genius are no longer reflected for many in standard American education. In the wartime leader's era, the Greek language was commonly taught at British and American universities as were the Greek classics. Younger students also had a knowledge of ancient Greece and its legacy. Today, most college students will never read Plato or Aeschylus, let alone study Athenian history or contemporary Greece and its place as a steadfast American ally, member of the European Union, the NATO defense alliance, and the global community. This publication will help correct that problem.

What you're reading does not pretend to be a scholarly, academic undertaking. It is nothing more or less than a report of Greek accomplishments I have encountered in over half a century of being immersed in Hellenic matters. I grew up in a Greek American community so proud that it claimed that Alexander the Great sent a ship east from India to California, making the Greeks the first to discover America. Much as my people may have enjoyed the image of the Greek leader coming ashore in Malibu, it wasn't so. Therefore, I approach each claim of Greek triumph with skepticism. You can rest assured, therefore, that the information reported here has been checked with highly reputable sources.

It is my humble hope that information in this book can help some readers make life choices that might make their lives better. It is meant to be an unofficial analysis and exploration of one nationality and is meant in no way to reflect badly on any other.

My Jewish friends should realize that my references about Greeks as a nationality leaves Jews out of the comparison. This is because much of the data compares only by nationalities and the Jewish community is divided among the Russian, Polish, Lithuanian, Ukrainian, and others.

Section I

CHAPTER 1

Who Qualifies to be Greek— Blood Helps but You Don't Have to Have It

Many Americans and even some Greek Americans do not understand fully what it means to be Greek or a Hellene. Many do not realize where the term Hellenism, meaning the culture of Greece, originates. It derives from an ancient prince of central Greece named Hellen, the son of Deucalion and Pyrrha. The Greeks became known as Hellenes and Greece as Hellas.

Is being Greek the result of DNA, the Greek way of life, or some other factor? Isocrates, a lesser known Greek philosopher, expressed his view on this subject when he said, "Being Greek is not so much a term of birth as it is of mentality."

This is a wise observation—one that holds as true today as it did 2,500 years ago. Science upholds the proposition. DNA testing supports Isocrates' contention. Many Greeks whose families have, for generations, believed that they were 100 percent Greek have learned through genetic testing that they are 65 percent, 50 percent Greek—or less. But this should come as little surprise. After all, if we count going back to our fourth great grandparent, we will find that we have 64 ancestors just there and each could have a claim to our DNA. And since 1780, we each personally have had over 1,000 direct ancestors. It's no wonder there are Greek prime ministers, Greek shipping magnates, and Greek American leaders who have technically been only half Greek or less.

Military occupation added to the complicated, mixed blood of so many Greeks. The Romans (the ancient Italians), the Venetians (the Italians from Venice), and the Ottomans (the Turks)—all conquered Greek lands. What's more, Greece has been at the heart of trade routes for millennia leading to more intermarriage and births. So, the likelihood of some of our family hailing from other countries is extremely high.

No matter! We welcome all who wish to be part of the Greek family. Interestingly, many Hellenes, regardless of the Greek percentage in their DNA, attribute their successes to their Hellenism. My career has taken me from being the youngest White House advance man, the youngest US Senate committee staff director, to the youngest assistant secretary in our government. It has equipped me to advocate for causes around the world and work with some of its most successful people. I have known many who saw themselves as Hellenes and attributed their success to Hellenism but had mothers or fathers without a drop of Greek blood in them. Hellenes seem to be Hellenes despite what many of their chromosomes may say.

CHAPTER 2

Numerous Areas Where Greeks Are Unsurpassed

Minoans and the Golden Age—A thousand years before the wheel came to some continents, the people of Greece measured the circumference of the earth within 10 percent accuracy

The Golden Age of Greece was further before the birth of Jesus Christ than we are after it today—3,000 compared to our 2,022. But more than 5,000 years ago, Greeks on the island of Crete created an indoor toilet that can work today. I refer to the Minoan civilization, named after the mythical King Minos of Crete. This is considered by some to be the Greeks' first major breakthrough in the civilization of humankind.

Whatever enabled the Greek-Minoan-Cretans to accomplish that incredible leap forward in humankind apparently carried forth through Hellenism. Roughly 2,500 years and 83 generations after the Minoans in 480 BC, the Golden Age of Greece arose, and the Greek people again did the seemingly impossible.

It is still hard to understand how the Greeks of the Golden Age working with only sticks, rocks, and dirt could measure the circumference of the earth within 10 percent accuracy, discover the existence of the atom, create what is considered to be the world's first computer—the Antikythera mechanism—and invent the formula that enables the measurement

3

of the distance to the moon and the sun, not to mention the size of these heavenly objects. Scholars at Cambridge University believe that a large number of precisely crafted interlocking bronze gears contained within the Antikythera mechanism that so accurately predicted a multitude of complex celestial movements were not lost to history. They now believe those gears in a simplistic form passed through the "Middle Ages" through the Islamic world, to the monasteries of Europe, and then to Germany where they were copied in the 1600s and emerged, roughly 1,700 years later, as the modern world's complex inner workings of sophisticated mechanical clocks.

The Greeks were the first to develop modern medicine, democracy, theater, and organized athletic competition. (Think of the Olympics.) But few realize that they also invented a long list of breakthroughs that moved us toward greater civilization. The internet is filled with lists of ancient Greek inventions. Even Wikipedia, the website that experts can correct, lists over 40.

The Greeks have been credited by some scholars to have been the first to develop something like a "middle class" between the very rich and the very poor. The Greeks believed the larger this middle group, the more stable the civilization.

These ancient Greeks developed the first trial by jury, civilians in government frequently controlled the military, and they had a *politea*, a sort of constitutional government giving civilians rights. They developed the original concept of individual rights (like free speech), free scientific inquiry, the study of philosophy, the careful recording of history, latitude and longitude, mathematics as a subject of study, the catapult, steam power, indoor heating and plumbing, the odometer, the alarm clock, the thermometer, the pulley, the crane, the lever, and the wheelbarrow. They were philosophers and technological innovators. Every one of these Greek creations has improved the lives of billions of people over time.

One hundred years after the Classical Period (or Golden Age), a Greek, Polybius, reached his zenith under Roman rule. He created the essential rule for a democratic constitution—the separation of power among governmental bodies and the checks and balances each governmental body can have on the others. He believed that, rather than trying to eliminate human nature's fundamental self-interest, we should use it to assure that no governmental body goes too far.

Creating the American System—Today's democracy was begun by the original Hellenes, echoed by America's Founding Fathers, and is now defended against the threat of extinction by descendants and students of our past

It is democracy that was arguably the most consequential invention of the Greeks of the Golden Age. Few realize that humankind's escape from oppression by kings and others falls into two time periods—for 250 years after ancient Greece's creation of democracy and again after America revived Greek democracy at the end of the 18th century.

The Greeks deduced that the only people who can hold power without violating their people's freedom are the people themselves. The Soviet and Chinese governments' murder of 20 million and 33 million of their people, respectively, in the 20th century validates this core tenet of Greek political thought.

The Greeks proved the viability of their unheard-of, out-of-the-box, seemingly unmanageable concept of democracy for non-slave,

adult males in Athens. And as their seed grew around the world, democracy grew to cover all adult citizens.

Greece's Golden Age in Athens took place over 1,000 years before the British stopped living in tribes, speaking predominantly non-English languages. And, there is another way to understand how truly profound the accomplishments of the ancient Greek Athenians were.

Global population at that time topped 150 million, according to modern estimates. Thucydides, the Greek historian, estimated the number of Athenian citizens to be only 40,000. That's fewer people than live in Cheyenne, Wyoming. The number of Greeks in Athens made up only 1/3750th of the global population at that time and yet they changed so much of the world.

Unfortunately, the Greeks of Athens were only able to maintain their democracy for 250 years (perhaps an ominous number as the US approaches the 250th anniversary of the Declaration of Independence). It was the military victory of Sparta, also part of Greece, over Athens, that started democracy's fall. Alexander the Great's father, Philip, finished off democracy by taking away control of the government from the people of Athens.

It is quite likely that none of these hundreds of breakthrough inventions for humankind would have occurred during the Golden Age were it not for Greek Spartan King Leonidas and his storied 300 Spartans (which has been portrayed in films like *300*) which preceded them. Had their small number not stepped forward to take on the 150,000-man army of Persian King Xerxes, the Greek seeds of Western civilization would never have been planted.

"Our arrows will block out the sun," boasted Xerxes. Leonidas' reply lives through the ages: "Then we shall have our battle in the shade." But when Leonidas realized that Xerxes' massive force had outmaneuvered him, the Spartan leader bravely sent the vast majority of his troops away to keep them safe. He and 300 men accepted certain death and remained in order to delay Xerxes.

The 300 Spartans defended their advanced Greek culture even though it meant their deaths. The plaque at Thermopylae where the 300 took their stand reads,

Go tell the Spartans, thou who pass by, that here, obedient to their laws, we lie.

In the wake of the 300 Spartans sacrificing themselves at Thermopylae, the greatly outnumbered Greek Navy under Athenian General Themistocles was able to defeat Xerxes at the Battle of Salamis. They kept the potential of the incredible creations of the Greek Golden Age from being destroyed before it was born.

Hellenism and its culture of excellence underpinned the rise chronologically throughout history of the Greek Minoan civilization on Crete, the Spartans at Thermopylae, and the Greeks of Athens during the Golden Age. That Hellenic wisdom's democracy advanced forward another 2,000 years to create the governmental essence of the most powerful nation the world had ever known—America.

Hellenism Led Our American Founders

Few realize that many of America's Founding Fathers learned to read and speak Greek, and all studied the Hellenic tradition. Thomas Jefferson, John Adams, Aaron Burr, Alexander Hamilton, Benjamin Franklin, and Thomas Paine, among others, made Hellenism their lodestar as they shaped the modern world's Greek democracy. George Washington, whose father died when he was 11, had his education interrupted and learned the wisdom of the Greeks through Greek translations.

The depth of our Founders' devotion to Hellenism can be seen in Jefferson's words, "I read one or two newspapers a week, but with reluctance give even that time from Homer." They were so familiar with the Ancient Greeks that Hamilton (of Broadway fame) would sometimes use the pseudonym Falchion—a 4th century BC Athenian found in Plutarch's *Lives*. The Founders filled their homes with paintings and busts of Homer, Socrates, and other Greek sages. In 1776, Adams wanted the engraving of the *Judgment of Hercules* (a powerful Greek myth depicting the choice between a life of pleasure or one of hardship and honor) as the Great Seal for the United States. Adams, the person who would go on to be America's second president, also used the Greek people's example as the justification for the revolt from England and the rule of King George III. He wrote, "The Greeks planted colonies and neither demanded nor pretended any authority over them."

America revived this unique form of government in the modern world and has kept it alive for nearly the same length of time as the ancient Greeks—250 years, as mentioned above. And, as we reach that 250-year mark in 2026, there is growing concern that we, too, may not be able to sustain it. The highly regarded World Values Survey data found that 70 percent of young Americans and a majority of Americans under the age of 60 do not think it is "absolutely essential" to live in a democracy.

Well-known Hellenes in America and famous American philhellenes (lovers of Greek culture) are fighting to maintain this gift of Hellenism's democracy. They initiated a behind-the-scenes effort to reinstill American faith in democracy. George Marcus, Dennis Mehiel, George Logothetis, and Manatos and Manatos created the American Democracy Month Council. Its primary purpose is to enlist US senators and members of the House in the effort to reeducate the American people about the necessity of democracy. The group enacted legislation specifically identifying today's loss of faith in democracy and also identifying the restoration of that faith as an official American goal. They are also moving senators and members to communicate pro-democracy messages to their tens of millions of daily social media followers.

The Council includes within it a bipartisan group of four former US Senate Majority Leaders—the now late Robert Dole, George Mitchell, Tom Daschle, and Trent Lott—and already has recruited the proactive involvement of 59 senators. Other Greek Americans involved are (alphabetically) former mayor of San Francisco, Art Agnos; University of Virginia Miller Center director and CEO and former White House assistant, Bill Antholis; the confidant of Ecumenical Patriarch Bartholomew and former American Archdiocese vicar general, Father Alex Karloutsos; former White House assistant and Ambassador, Tom Korologos; former Ambassador and Lt. Governor of California, Eleni Kounalakis; former Director of National Intelligence and Deputy Secretary of State, John Negroponte;

leading businessman and philanthropist, John Pappajohn; former president of the University of South Carolina, Harris Pastides; former US Senator Olympia Snowe; president of NowThis, Athan Stephanopoulos; television host, political commentator, and former top White House assistant, George Stephanopoulos; and television commentator and former top White House Homeland Security advisor, Frances Fragos Townsend.

Greeks in America Bottom to Top—Greeks who came to America in the early 1900s rose from the bottom to the top in one generation

At the turn of the 20th century, the immigration of Greeks to the United States dramatically accelerated. Like other immigrants, they were seeking a better life here. But, unlike many others, they were still reeling from nearly 400 years of Ottoman occupation. The Greeks who came to America in the early 1900s were poorly educated. A 19-year-old Greek male, like my grandfather, with five years of schooling, was considered highly educated. In many villages of Greece at the turn of the 20th century, there were no schools and many girls, like my grandmothers, received no education outside the home. As a result, many of the immigrant Greek American women and many men could not only not read English, but they couldn't read Greek either.

Many of the early, uneducated immigrant women spoke only Greek in their Greek enclaves. When they and many of their husbands tried to speak English, what came out was sometimes called "Grenglish," English with a Greek accent. For example, car in Greek is "aftokinitou" but many in that immigrant generation, always rolling their "Rs," called it "caro" and for train "traino." The pronunciation of American cities with their Greek/Cretan accents was interesting—Washington became "Vahshingtony, Salt Lake became "Soh-leh-chee" and for New York they used the Greek word for new and called it "Neo Yohkee."

We all wondered why after living in America for 50 years they still had such a thick accent. It wasn't until the late 1900s that science discovered that at around the age of 13 our brains lock into whatever

R.M.S. "CARPATHIA"

SALOON, CABIN, AND STEERAGE ALIENS MUST BE COMPLETELY MANIFESTED.

LIST OR MANIFEST OF ALIEN PASSENGERS FOR THE UNITED

Required by the regulations of the Secretary of Commerce and Labor of the United States, under Act of Congress approved February 20, 1907, to be delivered

S. S. _Athina_   sailing from _Piraeus_   _17 July_ 1910

17

accent we have. That means, if you moved to France when you were 11, once you learned the language they would think you were French. However, if you moved there at age 15, you would always sound like a foreigner.

Many friends in some other immigrant communities are very surprised when they learn that virtually every Greek who came to America in the early 1900s had nothing. They did not leave a prospering business or a business at all or possess a marketable skill. They were virtually all of the peasant class. At that time, during difficult economic conditions in Greece, roughly one out of every four young Greek males came to America hoping to secure a fortune and then return to Greece.

Initially, these immigrants' stories contained few great successes, like movie producer Spiro Skouras. During their first decades in America, the vast majority of Greek Americans worked as miners, waiters, and truck drivers or in modest businesses like candy stores, shoeshine stands, and hat blocking shops or famously in small restaurants and diners dotted across the American landscape. Some who ran hot dog stands by day taught themselves the stock market by night and made more money there than in their businesses.

Today many of these very small Greek restaurants have grown into major companies. And, in the New Jersey and New York area, a very high percentage of the many 24-hour diners are owned by Greek Americans.

These new Greek Americans largely stayed away from the criminal underworld that was so pervasive during Prohibition. The American Hellenic Educational and Progressive Association (AHEPA) even undertook a study of federal prisons in America to prove how few Greek Americans were imprisoned.

This does not mean that no Greek Americans dabbled in minor, nonviolent crime. During this time, a few Greek Americans, particularly in East Coast cities, participated in the nonviolent, yet unlawful "numbers racket"—taking bets on horse races. A few other Greeks were involved in gambling, legal and illegal. In the mid-20th century, if the average American was asked to name a famous gambler and odds maker, they likely would have said either "Nick the Greek" or "Jimmy the Greek Snyder" (originally Synodinos).

Also, a significant number of Greek immigrants continued making wine, primarily for their personal consumption, during Prohibition. As in the case of those in the numbers racket, very few were caught, very few went to jail, and those who did served only short sentences. Virtually all of these mostly young, petty criminal Greeks, particularly those in the numbers racket, displayed their Hellenic intelligence by investing these funds in legitimate businesses that in turn grew into great successes. This was certainly the case with numerous families in America's capital, Washington, DC.

Hellenism taught each of these early and very young Greek immigrants (even the gamblers) the importance of saving. Other Americans noted that even the poorest among the Greeks were very frugal. In addition to being careful with a nickel, their *philotimo* moved them to do more with their newly acquired money. According to academicians, sociologists, and authors Charles and Peter Moskos, between 1910 and 1930 these extremely poor immigrant Greeks sent over $650 million home to their families in Greece.

Uneducated though these first Greek Americans may have been, their Hellenism imparted valuable lessons. For example, a decade ago, the highly esteemed liberal Washington think tank, the Brookings Institution, revealed a path to economic success in America. Their 2013 study found that there is only a two percent chance of living in poverty and 77 percent chance of making at least $55,000 a year (equal to $70,000 in 2022) if people of all backgrounds (1) graduate from high school, (2) secure a full-time job, and (3) wait until they are 21 and married before having a baby. Seventy-nine percent of those who fail to do so are poor. The Hellenism of the Greek immigrants and their children drove them toward pursuing nearly all these goals mentioned.

There are some parts of non-Hellenic society that do not have the Greek frugality. One example is that of professional athletes. Reports of bankruptcies of professional athletes range widely, but CNBC reported in 2018 that 60 percent of NBA players go broke after five years and 78 percent of NFL players go bankrupt or are under financial stress just two years after retiring. According to Statista, in 2019, the average professional basketball and football player in America made an income on average of $8.3 million and

$3.2 million a year, respectively. The increased likelihood of avoiding financial catastrophes is one of the great gifts of Hellenism.

This Hellenic culture, mixed with the American culture in the early 1900s, formed an amalgam. It could be described as Greek drive and cleverness tempered by the kind of planning and preparation for which modern America and the ancient Greek coaches of the ancient Olympic greats were known. That amalgam of Hellenism and Americanism surpassed the Greeks in Greece and the Americans in America. Extraordinary vocational accomplishments of Greeks in America became more visible in the 1960s. In 1959, John Brademas became the first modern Greek American elected to the House of Representatives. In 1961, my father, Mike Manatos, became the first Greek American to work in a top position in the White House. And, at that time, many Hellenic doctors, lawyers, and businesspeople began to reach the upper echelons in their chosen fields.

From my father's position in the White House and my positions on the staff of US senators, I became acquainted with many of the rising Greek Americans and began to think that their numbers might be significant. I conducted a study of raw data from the 1970 census report to see if my impressions of our skyrocketing Greek American community were correct. At that time, because our immigrant generation very visibly still held low level jobs, major Greek Americans advised me that I would be disappointed by the census data I was going to analyze.

They were wrong. The data showed that immigrant Greek Americans ranked among the nationalities at the very bottom in terms of education and income. However, it showed that *American-born* Greek Americans in just one generation surpassed the education and income levels of virtually all American nationalities at that time.

And, what makes this accomplishment even more incredible, is that these Greek Americans did not do this—pass many other nationalities—in just any country. They did this in the 20th century's wealthiest and best-educated country in the world. Thus, this first generation of American-born Greeks compared extraordinarily well to the average levels of education and income of all the countries of the rest of the world.

There is another interesting aspect of this story. You see the Greeks who came to America and accomplished these wonderful things were not considered at the time in Greece to be the cream of Greece's crop. As mentioned earlier, they were considered to be peasants. Interestingly, many second-generation Greek Americans took great pride in that fact and considered it an egalitarian asset.

If the cream of Greece's crop had been the immigrants to America in the early 1900s, their success in this country would probably have been even greater. They, like those who did come, would not have suffered the first or the second Balkan Wars as well as the unimaginable ravages of WWII in Greece. Further, they would have come home after WWII to a relatively untouched nation on the verge of a historic economic boom.

All this verifies Churchill's earlier mentioned observation,

The passage of thousands of years sees no diminution in Greeks' original vitality.

For Greeks, education is of paramount importance. Greek children are taught from a young age that securing a significant education is an essential element for a good life. Greeks learned from the horrors of the 400-year Ottoman occupation that one's education is one of the few assets one can acquire that cannot be taken away. Greek immigrants took pride in the opportunity to join the world's educated class. Their admiration of education could be seen in several ways. For example, a high percentage of these immigrant children in America would go on to become teachers—the profession in Greece that was typically the most highly educated.

Two humorous stories about the sweet Greek immigrant mother of CIA Director George Tenet tell a part of the story. When George told his mother he decided not to go to law school, she said, "What am I going to tell the woman in church who I already told you were going to law school?" She then told George, as though she was trying to convince herself that she had not failed her children, "Well, after all your brother is a doctor."

Soon after George had been nominated to head the CIA, a lot of reporters were in his mother's tiny row house in Queens, New York, to interview her. She pulled out the baby pictures of George

and his brother Bill and said in her heavily Greek-accented English, "One a doctor, the other CIA director, not bad huh!" And to add to the picture of the innocence of that generation of proud Greek mothers, George's mother revealed her less than in-depth understanding of the operation of the CIA when she asked George's brother, "They are not going to send George into space, are they?"

The 1970 census data also showed other admirable characteristics of Greek Americans compared to other nationalities. These Greeks had the lowest levels of manual laboring and the highest levels of self-employment. The revelation that Greek Americans led in self-employment seemingly verified the frequent Greek American lament of years past, "we're too many chiefs and not enough Indians."

Greece today continues to be the wellspring of that productive ability. As a general rule, Greek-born Greek Americans tend to surpass American-born Greek Americans. This can be seen in the sciences, medicine, business, and in many other fields. Kyriakos

Mitsotakis, the prime minister of Greece elected in 2019, is himself an example of the wellspring of Greece. As an undergraduate at Harvard, one of the most prestigious American universities, his academic accomplishments surpassed 95 percent of all the other students in his class. He also excelled in graduate schools at Stanford and Harvard. His wife, also from Greece, did her graduate work at Harvard as well.

The positive result of this Hellenism is also apparent today in the economic success of Greeks in other vibrant economies. This evidence strongly suggests that if the Greek economy, saddled with high debt and other restraints, can itself become unfettered and merit-based, tremendous prosperity would come to the people in Greece. And by 2022, Mitsotakis attracted major high tech American companies to Greece. So hopefully, this is the beginning of that important change for Greece.

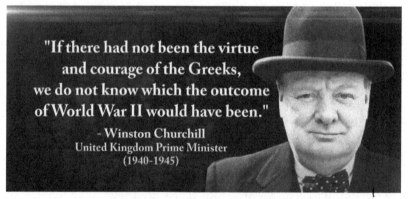

Proof That Greece Was Essential to the Defeat of Adolf Hitler's Evil

During World War II, the value of Hellenism showed itself again. In the middle of the night, an Axis Forces representative awakened the prime minister of Greece and, in effect, asked him to surrender as so many other countries had done. Prime Minister Ioannis Metaxas reportedly answered with one word that would become famous in Greece and among many others around the world—"*Oxi!*" or "No!" in Greek. The prime minister and the Greek people's courage was off the charts because they knew they were standing virtually alone

as they took on a monstrous evil they knew they could not defeat, Hitler's Axis Forces.

When Greece stood up to the Axis Forces in 1941, the Nazis had just defeated 14 countries including France, the world's most powerful military at the time. Just four months earlier Great Britain's military had been routed, sent into retreat, and only by pure chance not totally wiped out on the beaches of Dunkirk. The situation looked hopeless. America was not yet in the war. The Soviet Union had a nonaggression pact with Hitler. Little Greece, with help from weakened Great Britain, stood nearly alone against Hitler. Yet, like the outnumbered Spartans, the Greek people became the first allied force in Europe to beat back Hitler's Axis allies. US President Franklin Roosevelt exalted the Hellenic achievement,

When the entire world had lost all hope, the Greek people dared to question the invincibility of the German monster raising against it the proud spirit of freedom.

British Prime Minister Churchill also poetically said, "Hence, we will not say that Greeks fight like heroes but that heroes fight like Greeks."

More Nazis were killed on the first day the Germans parachuted onto the Greek island of Crete than had been killed on any single day in that year-and-a-half-old war. The men of Crete were fighting the Nazis on the mainland and only some British and New Zealand troops were left on the island with Cretan women who used pitchforks, shovels, old guns, knives, and whatever weapons they could find. The women killed so many Nazis that after the end of the 10-day battle that the Nazis ultimately won, they reportedly executed 1,000 Cretan women and sent another 500 to camps.

Some attribute this extraordinary action by the Cretan women to the fact that while most of Greece was liberated from the Ottoman occupation in 1828, Crete was still under some Turkish occupation until 1913. Thus, the Cretan women were only a few decades removed from living in a world where, for many, the rule was "kill or be killed."

Greece's initial defeat of the Axis Forces and the later battles with the Nazis in Greece did much to secure the victory in World War II. The Greeks delayed significantly Hitler's invasion of the Soviet Union. And it was the Soviet Union's punishing winter and military strength that reversed Hitler's string of victories and led to the beginning of the Fuhrer's defeat. The delay enabled the Soviets to recover from their recent war with Finland where they lost over 1,000 planes and tanks and hundreds of thousands of men and also to recover from Stalin's purge of his top military leadership.

Explaining Greece's impact, the Soviet Field Marshall Georgy Zhukov said,

> The Greek people delayed the German divisions during the time they could bring us to our knees.

And Soviet Premier Joseph Stalin himself said of the Greeks,

> You gave us time to defend ourselves.

At the post-war Nuremberg Trials, even Hitler's Field Marshall Wilhelm Keitel said of Greece's delay of the Nazis,

> If we did not have this long delay, the outcome of the war would have been different in the eastern front and in the war in general.

And, Churchill summed up the bottom-line effect that Greece had on the defeat of Hitler's Axis Forces when he said,

If there had not been the virtue and courage of the Greeks, we do not know which the outcome of World War II would have been.

This bravery of the Greek people at that pivotal moment in the history of humankind lifted their small number of seven million to stand with the world's powerhouses of the United States with 132 million people, the British Empire with control over 400 million, and the Soviet Union with 170 million. These four countries stopped Hitler's goal of world domination.

Without Greece, the world could well have experienced exterminations of unimaginable proportions. Hitler's already identified targets were the entirety of the Jewish people, the LGBTQ community, those with physical or mental disabilities, and people of African origin living outside of Africa. Today's world owes much to the people of Greece and the others who defeated Hitler.

Amazingly, history thus repeated itself yet again, for the third time a small number of Greek people were essential to the trajectory of Western civilization. First, there were the 300 Spartans. Next, there were the only 40,000 Greek citizens in Athens who created the broad and deep foundation for Western civilization with their inventions ranging from modern medicine to democracy. And third, it was the only seven million Greek people during WWII who were crucial to saving civilization.

Before leaving the subject of Greeks on the battlefield, you should know that the natural courage in Hellenes also showed itself during the Korean War in the 1950s. An American soldier in Korea who fought next to Greek soldiers wrote a book wherein he said that he found the Greeks to be different. He said that unlike all the other soldiers on the front line, when the fighting had paused, the Greeks uniquely were not particularly quiet as they partied among themselves. And when the fighting began, he said, the Greeks went after the North Korean and Chinese enemy far more aggressively than any of the other soldiers. This Greek courage was so apparent, he observed, that before attacking the front line, the enemy would first determine where the Greeks were located so that they could attack elsewhere.

Archbishop
of Greece
Damaskinos

Only the People of Greece Publicly Opposed the Holocaust as It Was Happening—Among all the Nazi-occupied countries of WWII

The reaction of the people of Greece to Hitler's attempt to exterminate the Jewish people shines a spotlight on Greek heroism, compassion, and kindness. Archbishop Damaskinos was the only national religious leader in a Nazi-occupied country to publicly oppose the Holocaust as it was happening. The Archbishop showed incredible courage in the face of the Gestapo general's reactive threat to put him before a firing squad, as the Nazis had with so many Greeks. The Archbishop responded to the threat by publicly saying, *"According to the traditions of the Greek Orthodox Church, our prelates are hanged and not shot. Please respect our traditions!"* The combination of the general's surprise and the Archbishop's extraordinary popularity with the population of Greece moved the general to spare the Archbishop's life.

On the Greek island of Zakynthos when Metropolitan Chrysostomos, the leading church official, and the mayor were told under the threat of death by the Nazis to submit the names of all the Jews on the island, the Metropolitan's reaction was also unprecedented. He instead sent the Jewish community to the mountain

Metropolitan
Chrysostomos
of Zakynthos

villages where they were all saved. He submitted to the Nazis a list containing only two names, his own and the mayor's.

In addition, across Greece, many Greek citizens risked and lost their lives hiding Jewish families from the Nazis. Most of those who hid Jews from the Nazis and the Jews being hidden were just typical Greek citizens. For example, one of my family members hid a Jewish family. When they were discovered, the Jewish family and my family member were killed. Some of those who hid the Jews and some of the Jews were notable figures. Monks in a Greek monastery hid the father of Shimon Peres who was fighting for the British in Greece. His son went on to become Israeli prime minister and Nobel Peace Prize winner.

The mother-in-law of Queen Elizabeth, who began her life as Princess Alice of Greece and became a Greek Orthodox nun later in life, risked death by hiding a Jewish family in her home across the street from Gestapo headquarters in Athens. Her son, His Royal Highness Prince Philip, the Duke of Edinburgh, in 2015 accepted in Buckingham Palace the Washington Oxi Day Foundation's Courage Award for Princess Alice, posthumously, presented by James Chanos of New York. That nonprofit foundation, which we created in 2011, recognizes those who today show the courage of the Greek prime minister who responded to the Axis Forces representative's request for Greece's surrender by saying "No," or "Oxi" in Greek. Others who have received awards from the Washington Oxi Day Foundation include President Joe Biden on behalf of his late son, Beau; as well as, journalist Maria Ressa and survivor of ISIS atrocities Nadia Murad, both of whom went on to receive Nobel Peace Prizes; another Nobel Prize winner Elie Wiesel; His All-Holiness Ecumenical Patriarch Bartholomew; and the late civil rights leader, Congressman John Lewis; among others.

A Jewish documentary video producer, Sy Rotter, interviewed Jews in Greece who were saved and the non-Jewish Greek people who courageously saved them. When those who saved Jews were asked why they did it, each answered with a variation of the statement that "the Jews were going to be killed," "it was something that had to be done," "it was nothing." Those Jews who were saved each described what it meant to them by saying some variation of the phrase "it was everything." The refrains were used so frequently that the Jewish video producer named the video "It Was Nothing—It Was Everything."

Try though the Greek people did to save their Jewish countrymen, over 50,000 Greek Jews died at Auschwitz. The National Holocaust Memorial Museum explains, "The Jewish community of Thessaloniki was highly concentrated in the city. Jews had no idea that they were going to killing centers; they believed the German subterfuge that they were going to work in Poland. Moreover, the controversial

Prince Philip, Duke of Edinburgh and James Chanos

German speaking Austrian head rabbi, Zvi Koretz, reportedly assisted the Germans in organizing efficient roundups. Because Ladino was the first language of Thessaloniki Jews, their spoken Greek was easy to distinguish. While the possibility of escape existed, most Jews, fearing separation from their families, did not take advantage of the available options."

While virtually all the Thessaloniki Jews were executed, the Nazis did not execute Rabbi Koretz or his family. He died after Auschwitz was liberated. Stuart Eizenstat, the special representative of President Bill Clinton for Holocaust-era issues, told me that he found that the Greeks compared favorably to other countries in terms of their handling of the property of Jewish people who were taken to concentration camps and never returned.

The Greek Jews in Auschwitz also displayed extraordinary Hellenic courage, carrying out the only revolt at the death camp. As they were being killed, they reportedly sang the Greek national anthem.

Sitting next to Holocaust survivor and Nobel Laureate Elie Wiesel at a dinner one evening, I mentioned that Greeks prided themselves on courage and principle. He went on to tell me that each group of Jews that arrived at Auschwitz was ordered to burn bodies of the dead. Each group said no and the Nazis then told them with machine guns in hand, "If you don't we will kill you now." Wiesel said that only one group, the Jews from Greece, told the Nazis, "Then kill us now."

In America the close relationship between the Greek and Jewish communities is apparent. For example, a Chicago Greek Orthodox priest told me some time ago that once a year in Chicago the priests, rabbis, and other religious leaders and lay leaders come together in fellowship. And he added that when the group breaks for lunch, the Greek Orthodox and the Jews tend to have lunch together at a far higher rate than they do with any other category of faith.

A Greek American high school student in the 1960s may have explained the relationship when he told the following to his Jewish friends. He said, "You know your people and mine seem to be trying to do the same things, although I must admit that your people seem to be doing it a little bit better than ours."

Nazi Concentration Camp

Intelligence and Wit of Greek American Political Leadership

Even among American politicians, Greek Americans have stood out for their intelligence among some of America's most successful people. For instance, Congress in the 1970s was made up of many of America's top citizens including three Rhodes Scholars. They were the Speaker of the House Carl Albert and two Greek Americans—Congressmen Paul Sarbanes (D-MD) and John Brademas (D-IN).

Although Greek Americans made up less than one half of one percent of the American population, we made up 66 percent of the Rhodes Scholars in the Congress. As an aside, Hellenes George Stephanopoulos, a top aide in the Clinton White House, and Sylvia Mathews Burwell, President Barack Obama's Secretary of the Department of Health and Human Services, are Hellenic Rhodes Scholars as well.

Brademas went on to very nearly become the Speaker of the US House of Representatives, the third in rank in the American government. However, our community had not yet become adequately sophisticated to understand that he could only stay in office if he raised significant funds to purchase enough television advertising time to tell his story. In this regard, our community failed him, and unfortunately in 1980, he was defeated for reelection. Had he not suffered that defeat, he was in line, just behind Speaker Jim Wright, to become the next Speaker of the House.

Paul Tsongas

Paul Sarbanes

John Brademas

George Stephanopoulos

Sylvia Mathews Burwell

Olympia Snowe

Nick Galifianakis

Before leaving the House, 41-year-old Sarbanes was selected by the House Judiciary Committee to draft the language for that committee's most important actions of that era—the Articles of Impeachment for President Richard Nixon. He was chosen because of the high regard in which his intelligence and integrity were held by both Democrats and Republicans. Following his service in the House, Sarbanes became the first Greek American to be elected a United States senator. This was for the national Greek American community a major recognition of our Americanness. Every Greek, Democrat or Republican, felt great pride in this accomplishment.

Senator Sarbanes was known for his major legislative victories. Possibly, the best-known was the major reform in corporate executive responsibility for financial wrongdoing—the "Corporate and Auditing Accountability, Responsibility, and Transparency Act," commonly known as the Sarbanes-Oxley Act. Prior to that act, laws controlling corporate conduct were lax. That became particularly exposed in the historic scandal that caused the collapse of the Enron Corporation. Its stock price fell from $90.75 to $0.26 per share, thousands of employees became unemployed, and it devastated its retirement plan. It was described as "shaking Wall Street to its core." Sarbanes' legislation put an end to the highly dishonest practices that caused this debacle.

For decades Senator Sarbanes was the go-to expert on matters relating to the Ecumenical Patriarchate, Greece, and Cyprus. His position on the Senate Foreign Relations Committee, the institution that must approve all major positions in the State Department, significantly increased the impact he had on American policy toward these subjects.

Sarbanes also individually made history at Princeton University where he was the only graduate in the school's history to have won its highest undergraduate recognition, the Pyne Honor Prize, and later have one of his sons go on to receive that prize as well.

Sarbanes was followed to the US Senate by only two other Hellenes—Senator Paul Tsongas (D-MA) and Senator Olympia Snowe (R-ME). Tsongas was a Democrat even though his parents were quite conservative. He used to jokingly say when his parents got off the boat, a fortune-teller told them she had good news and bad news about a son they would have. In answer to his mother's question about the good news, the fortune-teller said, "He will be elected to the United States Senate." In answer to the question about the bad news, she said, "He will be a Democrat."

Sarbanes was clearly one of our country's most brilliant people and one day at Princeton he had a chance encounter with arguably the most brilliant. While studying in his dormitory room where his window was about 10 feet above a campus sidewalk, Sarbanes was interrupted by a very nearby loud conversation. He called out asking the speakers to quiet down. The loud talking continued, so he called out again in a louder voice. It continued, so he rose from his desk to tell the loud talkers below his window to be quiet. He was shocked to see that one of the loud talkers was Albert Einstein.

Another Greek American member of the House of Representatives who served with Brademas and Sarbanes was Nick Galifianakis (D-NC). (His nephew is the famous comedian and actor, Zach Galifianakis.) Nick is pretty funny himself and had some things to say about his scholarly colleagues Sarbanes and Brademas. He used to play the role of a "country bumpkin," although he was previously a law professor at Duke University. In his thick Southern accent, Galifianakis used to like to joke in remarks at Greek American events,

"Brademas graduated Magna Cum Laude, Sarbanes graduated Magna Cum Laude, and I graduated 'Thank the Laude'."

The Hellenic trail in Congress, blazed by Brademas and Sarbanes, continues. In the vast majority of years, the percentage of US senators and members of the House who are Hellenes, including Paul's son Congressman John Sarbanes, is equal to or greater than the half percent we represent in America.

Numerous Greeks did extraordinarily well in the US Congress. Probably the most admired Congressional action of the last century was the enactment of the Civil Rights Act of 1964 and the Voting Rights Act of 1965. The biggest hurdle that legislation had to overcome was in the US Senate which was then controlled by southern senators who were the legislation's greatest opponents. President Lyndon Johnson had my father, Mike Manatos, lead the White House effort to enact those bills in the Senate. His relationships with senators of both political parties, his diplomacy, and his Hellenic drive helped pass those historic and once considered doomed bills.

As of the writing of this book in 2022, we have no Hellenic senators. Hellenes who followed their House service with becoming senator include Sarbanes, Tsongas (who also gave President Clinton strong competition for the Democratic presidential nomination in 1992), and Snowe. And the current Hellenic members of the US House of Representatives include (in order of seniority) John Sarbanes (D-MD), Gus Bilirakis (R-FL), Dina Titus (D-NV), Charlie Crist (D-FL), Chris Pappas (D-NH), and Nicole Malliotakis (R-NY). Hellenes who served in the House following Brademas include Sarbanes, Snowe, Tsongas, Peter Kyros (D-ME), Gus Yatron (D-PA), Skip Befalis (R-FL), Nick Mavroules (D-MA), George Gekas (R-PA), Mike Bilirakis (R-FL), Shelley Berkley (D-NV), Ron Klink (D-PA), Zack Space (D-OH), and Niki Tsongas (D-MA).

Greek Americans have made their mark in the White House too—holding the positions of chief of staff more than once. John Podesta had the top job for President Clinton and Reince Hercules Priebus did for President Donald Trump. Also, at one time, all four deputy chiefs of staff were Greek Americans. They included Burwell who, as mentioned earlier, went on to become secretary of the Department of Health and Human Services and Podesta who went on to become White House chief of staff. For meetings, the chief of staff at that time would tell his personal assistant to "bring the Greeks in." This selection of Greeks for such top-level White House positions could not be the result of pure chance.

The first Greek American to be elected vice president was Spiro Agnew. He was Nixon's first vice president, elected in 1969. For Agnew, Hellenism was not revered. Born in 1918, he spent his formative years amid the recently immigrated Hellenes, most of whom held menial jobs and spoke broken English. It was an era when my parents as children, for example, were called "dirty Greeks." There was a very small percentage of Greek Americans who were less than proud of being identified with these low status Americans. Agnew was among them. He may have inherited that view from his father who was one of only three percent of the early Greek immigrants to marry a non-Greek.

The vast majority of Greek Americans were not proud of him once they learned of his view of our heritage. In 1973 when Agnew was charged with bribery and was dropped from the vice presidency, Greek Americans felt little pity for him. It is unfortunate that he forgot the best of Hellenism's lessons at a time he and our country most needed them.

Record Setting in Washington, DC—Legislatively, personally, and operationally, Greeks have set many records in the White House and the Congress of the United States

What follows describes some historic accomplishments of Greek Americans in Washington, DC, where I watched the Greek American ascension and can provide behind-the-scenes points of interest. The first two occurred when I was a relatively young staffer in the US Senate.

In the US Senate, intense opposition to a bill can kill it with what is called a "filibuster." A filibuster can only be overcome by invoking what is called "cloture." It requires securing the votes of two-thirds of the 100 US senators. By 1973, overriding a filibuster had only been accomplished 16 times in our country's nearly 200-year history. With the confidence and drive that my Hellenic culture passed on to me, as a US Senate staff person, I led the floor fight for the postcard voter registration bill and invoked cloture for only the 17th time.

The next example involves the only time in modern history the Congress overruled the White House on a major foreign policy issue. It was a long and difficult legislative fight, but after 12 different congressional votes in numerous committees and on the floor of both the House and Senate, the Greek Americans won and stopped US arms deliveries to Turkey, which had illegally used American arms to invade and occupy Cyprus in 1974. It was an honor to lead that lobby effort from my position on the staff of Senator Thomas Eagleton, a great philhellene who introduced a bill to cut off aid to Turkey.

Right was certainly on the side of the Greek American community. American law was very specific with respect to terminating US military aid to any country which used our arms aggressively. In 1974, Turkey, a country of 38 million, using American-supplied planes and other weapons, invaded Cyprus, a country of 600,000. They captured 1,000 Greek Cypriots and five American citizens including a 16-year-old boy vacationing there with his family. Within two days of the capture, they dug mass graves and executed each of the men, women, and children. Turkey hid these executions from America for 20 years. It was discovered only when the Greek American community worked with newly elected Congressman Eliot Engel to pass a law through the House and Senate demanding our State Department find out what Turkey had done with these captives.

Following the invasion, President Nixon and Secretary of State Henry Kissinger decided to ignore American law and continue sending arms to Turkey. Many on Capitol Hill were shocked in light of the fact that this ignoring of American law occurred as Nixon was being highly criticized for lack of adherence to US law in the Watergate incident.

Nixon and Kissinger's disregard for the law to cut off aid to Turkey for its invasion of Cyprus has played a role in Turkey's subsequent illegal actions. Soon after the invasion, the Turkish military began its occupation of the northern third of Cyprus, a western democracy and ally of the United States. That illegal occupation continues to this day, nearly half a century later.

By the time my boss, Senator Eagleton, had introduced the bill to cut off aid to Turkey, Greek Americans Sarbanes , Kyros, Yatron, and Bafalis had joined Brademas in the US House of Representatives. While Brademas and Sarbanes led the fight for the arms embargo in the House, they were backed by a Greek American community across the country that had grown tremendously in stature. Were it not for the extremely high regard for Brademas and Sarbanes, we would not have won some of the close votes. Also, without the state by state, congressional district by congressional district communications of Greek Americans with their elected representatives, directed from the Senate and elsewhere in Washington, we never could have beaten the White House.

Prior to Turkey's invasion of Cyprus, the national profile of Greek Americans was not high. Even Vice President Nelson Rockefeller, the former governor of New York—a state with a huge Hellenic population—showed his poor understanding of us Greeks. He once expressed his displeasure with actions of the citizens of Greece by saying something to the effect that "they should pray to whichever God it is they pray to."

When the first vote involving the Turkish arms embargo was cast on the US Senate floor in 1974, we mentioned to a senator from Pennsylvania, Richard Schweiker, that if he voted yes to the aid cutoff, his Greeks in Pennsylvania would be very pleased. His response to me was, *"I don't have any Greeks in Pennsylvania,"* when in fact there were large communities in Philadelphia, Pittsburgh, and in some towns. Many weeks later, by the end of all 12 votes on Capitol Hill, Schweiker and the other 99 senators and 435 members of the House knew full well just how many Greeks they had as constituents.

Prior to these votes on Turkey's invasion and occupation of Cyprus, the Greek American community was divided along many lines. Those differences split between the right or the left, between prior supporters of Prime Minister Eleftherios Venizelos or King Constantine

I, membership in the AHEPA or the GAPA (The Greek American Progressive Association), and between churches or one organization representing the Greek American community in Washington against another.

At the first meeting of the heads of all the organizations I called in the US Senate, one leader stomped out of the room and told me he refused to be in the same room with someone who supported the recently fallen military regime in Athens. Others expressed the same thing about others thought to be, but were not in American terms, communists. I explained to the group that we had no chance whatsoever of reversing the White House on the Turkish invasion of Cyprus unless we all pulled together. Given those circumstances, that meeting proceeded constructively and our national community united and since that time, the old rivalries for which our community had once been famous dramatically subsided.

Many months before anyone thought that Turkey might invade Cyprus, I met with other Hellenes who had some Washington experience. We discussed the creation of an organization to represent our community in Washington. From the US Senate, I had seen up close the value of the Jewish lobby to that community and other such Washington organizations representing interest groups. For many weeks Gene Rossides, a Washington lawyer and former assistant secretary of the treasury, and I had been jointly writing a structure and bylaws for such an organization. When the invasion occurred, Rossides quickly filed it as the American Hellenic Institute (AHI) and submitted an excellent legal brief in support of congressional action.

This invasion and effort to enforce US law embargoing US arms to Turkey organized our community from a hardly heard of community into a national powerhouse. We emerged in America as a group not to be toyed with. In the early months of the effort to impose the embargo from Senator Eagleton's office, I was happy to write most of the various groups' material and directed their targeting of senators and members. Rossides called me at 8:00 a.m. on the morning that a major *Washington Post* article about the power of the new "Greek Lobby" was published. He wanted to apologize before I read the article where he claimed for AHI and himself the work I had done for them. I told him I had no problem whatsoever—it made our community look that much more significant to the representatives still voting on the issue.

We worked as well with the AHEPA. They were on the phones for months calling each of their chapters and instructing them how to lobby their senators and members. And the most effective entity for this effort was the over 500 Greek Orthodox churches across the country and our impressive Archbishop Iakovos. Senators and members listen far more closely to individuals who have a following of a few hundred of their constituents, as priests do.

There is another record we set that was considered impossible to achieve. It involved Appropriations Subcommittee Chairmen who years ago had such dominating power over their subcommittee they had never been beaten on a vote by them. These Chairmen had such power they enjoyed being called the "College of Cardinals"—the name of the Catholic hierarchs who choose the next pope.

However, Cyprus was in such a dangerous situation we decided to take on an Appropriations Subcommittee Chairman in our effort to get Turkey off Cyprus. We threatened to cut $100 million from the $1 billion a year the US was giving Turkey in foreign aid unless they ended their occupation of Cyprus. Every single member of that subcommittee who we pushed hard to vote for our amendment to cut $100 million in Turkish aid said something to the effect, "I will vote with you, but there is no chance we can beat the Chairman." Our secret weapon on that subcommittee was the chairman of another subcommittee. We strongly activated several important Hellenic friends in his Congressional district. When the vote was taken, the other chairman on that subcommittee who we had lobbied intently said "present" instead of "no" to our amendment and, as a result, our amendment passed. Everyone was shocked—we had done the impossible. After that victory, the Chairman gave up and each year supported our amendment to cut another $100 million from Turkey's aid. And, after cutting an annual $100 million from that Turkish foreign aid for a few years, we cut it to zero.

Although it did not set a record, another policy accomplishment was very important to Cyprus. It occurred during President Clinton's Administration. Officials and citizens in Cyprus at all levels frequently said that it was just a matter of time before Turkey moved to take the rest of the island. We alerted the newly appointed Assistant Secretary of State for Europe, Dick Holbrooke, with whom I had worked in the Carter Administration, about this danger to Cyprus. He had just left the post of Ambassador to Germany when we told him that if Germany and France did not object to it, Cyprus could begin early European Union (EU) accession talks and that Turkey would not dare attack an EU country. Within weeks of our discussion Holbrooke was on a plane to Germany and France, moving them both to withdraw their objections. Once those accession talks began, no one spoke of Turkey taking the rest of the Island.

In the late 1990s, our national Greek Orthodox Archdiocese in New York—under the leadership of our Archbishop and carried out by Father Karloutsos—and our Orthodox priests across America worked with our firm to assure that the US Congress would appropriately recognize our Ecumenical Patriarch Bartholomew, the spiritual father of Orthodox Christians, the second largest Christian church worldwide. As a global leader in faith, peace, and the environment, it would be only appropriate for him to receive the highest award presented by Congress, the Congressional Gold Medal reserved for leaders like Washington and Churchill. To receive this award, the resolution of nomination needed the co-sponsorship of two-thirds of the senators and members of Congress. As a result of His All-Holiness' sterling record of accomplishment and the devotion of our community to him, we secured such a large number of co-sponsors that we tallied more than any other of the more than 1,000 bills introduced in the Congress that session. He received the award in 1997.

We Greeks also set the record with respect to the utilization of the world-famous US Capitol and its marvelous Rotunda—the huge open space under the Capitol dome. As an aside, the great paintings adorning the walls of the US Senate and the dome of the Capitol building were the work of Constantino Brumidi, who lived from 1805 to 1880 and was a Greek/Italian American.

In 1990, the US Capitol Building and its Rotunda were 190 years old and used for presidents "lying in state" after their death. However, working in close coordination with Father Karloutsos, we were able to move the then Speaker of the House and friend, Tom Foley, to allow our Ecumenical Patriarch, who at the time was Demetrios (the predecessor of Bartholomew), to use the Rotunda for a ceremony. It was only the second time in American history that it was used for a living person. There were many other nationalities and other powerful interest groups in the US at the time that would have very much liked to have had their event in the Rotunda, but it was only us Greek Americans who were first to secure it in modern times. As is the case throughout history for the Greeks, these things did not happen by chance.

Annual Meeting with the US President—Only the Greeks (1 of 250) able to achieve what the Irish (1 of 8) achieved— a meeting with every president every year for 33 years

Greeks achieved another significant distinction in America, meeting with every president each year for over 33 years. Only one other nationality group, the Irish, has been able to do it successfully. This is a particularly significant accomplishment for Greek Americans because the Irish make up one out of every eight Americans, giving

White House meeting with President George H.W. Bush

them obvious power. However, Greek Americans accomplished this same meeting while making up only one out of every 250 Americans.

Virtually every president or prime minister of the 194 foreign countries and virtually every one of the 535 US senators and members of the House and virtually every one of the 50 governors of every state and every one of the thousands of heads of every major business or labor or other American organization want to plead his or her case personally to the president. They would love to do this once, let alone every year. The most powerful organizations in Washington with budgets of over $30 million a year are unable, with rare exceptions, to accomplish such routine face-to-face meetings with the president.

The White House celebrates Irish Americans on St. Patrick's Day and the White House celebrates Greek Americans on Greek Independence Day. This annual event began with our passage of a resolution through the US Senate and House in 1987 and includes all the presidents since—Ronald Reagan, George H.W. Bush, Clinton, George W. Bush, Obama, Trump, and Biden. In each case, we got a Greek American close to whichever president was in power to also urge the president to celebrate the resolution's passage with a White House event. Contrary to the misimpression of many, the event is not at all automatic and must be reestablished every year. It is particularly difficult to maintain when new presidents enter office with a promise to do things differently than all of their predecessors.

The high regard earned by Greek Americans in every community and for Greek Americans' leader, our Archbishop, is behind this accomplishment. But other ethnicities are also held in high regard and yet cannot secure such an annual White House meeting. The probable explanation for this Greek distinction lies in the fact that Hellenes are so proud of their culture, as surveys confirm, and take their Hellenism very personally—as something worth sacrificing for.

First Joint Meeting of Congress with a Prime Minister of Greece

In 2022, Speaker of the US House of Representatives Nancy Pelosi invited Greek Prime Minister Kyriakos Mitsotakis to be the first prime minister of Greece in history to make a presentation before a Joint Meeting of Congress. This is an event that carries with it all the ceremony of US Presidents' State of the Union addresses. Speaker Pelosi is considered by Democrats, including myself, to be the best Speaker of the House in modern history. As well, she is considered by many of our Republican friends who disagree with her policies to be this era's most effective Speaker. Her intelligence, energy, charm, strength, and commitment to serve the public make her a rare woman of both velvet and steel.

Pelosi's very high regard for Prime Minister Mitsotakis, Greece, Cyprus, the Greek American community, and her concern about the fragility of democracy in America played a major role in her historic invitation. Her relationship with Hellenes goes back to her brother's friend in Baltimore, Ted Venetoulis, who took her to her senior prom. As a young intern in a Senator's office, she knew my father, Mike Manatos, during his White House days with President Kennedy. She has had decades of strong support and a close relationship with the Angelo Tsakopoulos family, including daughter Eleni Tsakopoulos Kounalakis, the current Lt. Governor of California; and billionaire real estate and restaurant mogul, George Marcus, and his wife Judy. Another Hellene, Dennis Mehiel of New York is also her longtime supporter and friend. As well, when first elected to represent San Francisco in the US Congress, she had a very close relationship with that city's Hellenic Mayor, Art Agnos. That is when I met and began working with her, as we were representing San Francisco in Washington, DC. Over the decades we have worked closely with her, securing from the Congress roughly $5 million a year for health clinics in Hellenic areas of the former Soviet Union and numerous other matters important to Greece, Cyprus, and the Greek American and Greek Orthodox community. Hellenes never have had and never will again have a better Speaker of the House.

Virtually all of these extraordinary Hellenic accomplishments in Washington, DC, that we have been in the middle of must recognize the importance of one individual in particular. I refer to the previously noted Father Karloutsos, the former vicar general of our national Archdiocese in New York. His intelligence and effectiveness are unsurpassed.

Greeks Number One in World in Marrying Mothers of Their Children

Family matters to all people, of course, but a 2018 international study by Statista found that the people of Greece have the world's highest rate of matrimony between natural fathers and mothers of children. Precise numbers are unavailable for the US, but Greek American commitment to the nuclear family is in clear contrast to many others in America where 40 percent of all children are born to unmarried mothers, according to the Centers for Disease Control.

The importance of a father's influence in a family is profound. As President Obama said in a June 2008 speech,

> *Children who grow up without a father are five times more likely to live in poverty and commit crime; nine times more likely to drop out of schools, and 20 times more likely to end up in prison.*

And a 2022 Gallup Poll in the US found that the rate of single mothers who have not had enough money to buy food needed by her family is 235 percent higher than all others.

Cultural Admiration of Their Culture Exceeds That of All Europeans

Most Greeks are aware that Hellenes see advantages in their culture, but few are aware of how it compares to other cultures. A Pew survey (2015–2017) of Europeans posed the question, "Do you consider your particular culture superior to others?" Answering affirmatively were 20 percent of Spaniards, 26 percent of Swedes, 36 percent of French, 45 percent of Germans, and 46 percent of British. The Greeks, however, stood out dramatically at 89 percent answering in the affirmative. Greek Americans are just as proud. As the following documentation demonstrates, that confidence is well deserved.

Philotimo: A Constellation of Greek Virtues—Only the Greek language needed a word, *philotimo*, for these virtues

There is a constellation of virtues that are practiced so widely and frequently by Greek people that the Greek language developed one word to describe them all—*philotimo*. As the pre-Socratic Greek philosopher Thales, who lived in the 500s BC, said,

> *Philotimo to the Greek is like breathing, a Greek is not a Greek without it.*

The concept of *philotimo* has been described as the best part of being Greek and the secret behind Greeks' success. The word breaks down as *philos* meaning "friend" and *timi* meaning "honor." It is commonly described as "the love of honor." But the word is so complex that it is nearly impossible to define outright. This love of honor has certainly played a role in Hellenism throughout history. It is seen in Greeks sacrificing their well-being and at times their lives for a greater good.

Nationally acclaimed newsman George Stephanopoulos described it,

> *like but going beyond the Golden Rule of doing to others as you would have them do to you.*

He continued, "It is doing that and then even doing more for that person than you would expect him or her to do for you." Another leader within the Hellenic community, the late businessman Ted Spyropoulos, said,

> *Philotimo is doing something for others without the expectation of anything in return except love and respect.*

An extraordinary example of *philotimo* and the degree of appreciation, respect, and obligation it engenders among Hellenes can be seen in the conduct of an uncle in America and his nephew living in Greece during very difficult times. In the 1950s and 1960s, the uncle, Sam Armatas of Denver, routinely sent his siblings and their children in Greece $5, $10, and $20 bills from America with a note of well wishes. Records show that over a 20-year period, it surpassed $200,000.

One of those nephews, Angelos Pangratis, would go on to become a senior European Union ambassador to numerous countries and the chargé d'affaires of the EU delegation to America. Unfortunately, the uncle was no longer alive when the nephew arrived in Washington for his high EU assignment. Yet, the nephew's *philotimo* moved him to travel alone all the way to Denver to visit his uncle's grave.

In the 1930s, '40s, and '50s, Greeks moved quickly up America's economic ladder. It equipped many Greeks in America to show great *philotimo* to those still having a hard time in Greece. After rising to success through his store that sold the miners everything from clothing to hardware to groceries near Utah's Bingham Canyon Copper Mine, George Adondakis shared for the rest of his life his profits with his partner who became permanently unable to work. Similarly, John Roumel of Washington, DC, who in the 1950s was denied a house purchase because he was Greek, shared his business profits with his partner who could no longer work, thus enabling him to put his sons through medical school. John's son, Theodore, was singled out as a top employee of the 79,000-person Department of Health and Human Services and John's granddaughter, Eleni, would go on to serve in the White House as a lawyer for Vice President Mike Pence and in 2020 she became the first Greek American woman appointed chief judge of a federal court.

Adondakis also brought a number of young people, relatives, and others over from Greece, providing them with everything necessary to receive a college education. He sent money to relatives in Greece and loved America so much that he said he felt honored to pay taxes! He was quite wealthy but showed great wisdom by not letting his children feel that they were wealthy, requiring them to do chores in order to receive an allowance.

Decades after he passed away in 1984, many people told his children that during their terrible economic trials, their father overlooked the collection of debts for things they purchased from his store. An admirable number of Hellenes of that generation, whose memory of poverty was fresh, were lenient in their bill collection from those under financial strain.

The inordinate amount of gratitude Hellenes typically show in response to being gifted by another's *philotimo* combines at times with Hellenes' abundance of enthusiasm to surprise non-Greeks in America's political world. One example involved my boss, Senator Eagleton, giving to his friend, a senator from Illinois, Adlai Stevenson III, a Senate floor amendment for the arms embargo on Turkey due to its illegal use of US arms. We knew we would win and knew that his Greek Americans in Chicago (then said to have the second largest Greek population in the world) would love him for it.

Right after his amendment was adopted, Stevenson returned to

Chicago and the next week returned to Washington and expressed his shock. The rather formal and staid senator said, "Not only did hundreds of cheering Greeks greet me at my airport gate, but they lifted me onto their shoulders and carried me while cheering all the way through the airport." Similarly, Vice President Walter Mondale said,

I crisscrossed the country during our [1976] Presidential campaign meeting with every group imaginable, but my Greek event in Chicago outdid all the others by far.

Such Greek enthusiasm is not uncommon. Helen Maroulis, who was born in the Washington, DC, area in 1991, became in 2016 the first American woman to win an Olympic gold medal in wrestling. As *Sports Illustrated* wrote,

After her win, she went to visit her father's childhood island of Kalamos in Greece. Her dad watched her arrival on video, emotions soaring. "Everyone on the island, all the people came down cheering her as the boat came in," he says. "Church bells were ringing, horns honking."

To see his daughter return to his homeland as an Olympic gold medalist filled him with pride. "I left this island when I was a little boy, when there was no electricity or running water on the island," he says, recalling how he had to learn a whole new world whcn he came to America, including learning to speak English. "And here comes my daughter, back to the island where I was born." Later, the Greek government honored her by putting her image on a postage stamp. Says her father, "They really love her there." They treated her as though one of their own family had won an Olympic gold medal.

To many Greeks, *philotimo* certainly seems to be the primary standard by which Greeks measure themselves and others. Many believe that to be known as an individual with *philotimo* is the greatest compliment a Greek can receive. Young Greeks who are not being particularly virtuous in their studies or are figuratively kicking a person while he is down may well hear the admonition in question form—"Don't you have any *philotimo*?"

One of Greece's most significant philanthropists and successful shipowners, George P. Livanos, exemplified *philotimo*. It was visible in many ways but one instance that stands out in my mind was when a group of five of us, including George, back in 1994 was entering the Maximos Mansion, Greece's White House, to meet with Prime Minister Andreas Papandreou. As we shook the prime minister's hand, I realized that George was delayed behind us. It turned out he was speaking to the person who had held the front door open for us. Knowing George, I realized that it was not unusual for this billionaire to pay such respect to the person holding the door. To Livanos in many ways the person holding the door was just as important as the prime minister. Livanos treated everyone with dignity. *Philotimo* is part of the reason that Greeks are highly regarded in every community in America.

Another example of the depth *philotimo* can reach in some Hellenes involves Andy Athens, a retired steel executive. After the fall of the Soviet Union, he visited some oppressed Hellenic minorities still living in the former Soviet bloc—Georgia, Armenia, and Ukraine. In some areas, the oppression had been so harsh that speaking Greek was forbidden and people who violated that law had their tongues cut out.

These people continued to suffer from a virtual absence of medical care and this neglect moved the steel executive to raise money for health clinics. As part of his effort, I was able to work with the US House and Senate in order to secure $5 million a year (in today's dollars) for these clinics. Once, as Andy was explaining the clinics to members on the House Appropriations Committee, I asked him to detail how grateful the recipients were for his help. As he began to discuss the degree of gratitude that had been expressed to him by those in need, he began to cry so hard that he could not finish. For a full five minutes, I had to explain the program while he recovered from the profound emotional toll of his empathy and kindness toward others less fortunate.

Philotimo shows itself in many aspects of Greek American conduct that is typical of most Hellenes. Two very different cases in the 1950s show a virtually universal Hellenic view at that time.

My father and our family of five were living in a two-bedroom, one-bathroom apartment that cost $60 a month, a modest amount even at that time, in a neighborhood where crime was on the rise in the 1950s. His father, a retired coal miner, and his wife's father, a small farmer, were very limited financially. He worked in the US Senate, where, at the time, a senator made $15,000 a year, and junior staff salaries were significantly less. He dreamed of someday being able to put together the princely sum of $6,000 required as a down payment for purchasing a modest home in a safe neighborhood selling for $24,000.

At that time, the American government was deporting a wealthy Greek shipowner living in New York. His lawyer offered Dad tens of thousands of dollars to introduce legislation that would enable his client to remain in America. Granting this request was not as difficult as it would sound. At the time, if a noncitizen had legislation pending in the Congress that would enable him or her to remain in America, even though not enacted, he or she could not be deported. They called such bills, which were not uncommon, "ship-jumper" bills.

Dad assumed that his senator would not want to introduce such legislation. However, the Senate rules at that time allowed a senator's staff person to draft a bill and hand it to the Clerk of the Senate, thus formally introducing it. It was frowned upon but there was nothing illegal about it.

While many less ethical people in his financial situation would have taken the money, such acceptance would have violated his *philotimo*. After all, *philotimo* means the love of honor. Dad missed the chance to be wealthy but remained quietly proud of his Hellenic virtues.

An older woman we knew only as Mrs. Manos displayed another aspect of *philotimo* in 1960. She was quite different than Greeks who have immigrated to the US today. She arrived as a young adult, had minimal education, and depended on her significantly older husband. Her children were raised and married with families of their own.

Her children's incomes were not expansive, and her husband died, leaving her very little. She lived in a small, inexpensive apartment in a

Washington, DC, neighborhood with rising crime. Her situation was replicated many times by other old Hellenic immigrant women in the 1950s. Their financial situation qualified these women for significant housing and food assistance if they simply went on welfare. To a person, these Hellenic women's vision of honor would not allow them even to consider welfare. Their *philotimo* would not allow it.

Paul Sarbanes, the longest serving US senator in the history of the state of Maryland, also exemplified this humble and giving mindset. His *philotimo* moved him to treat all of his colleagues—Republicans, Democrats, liberals, and conservatives—with respect and humility. As a result, he enjoyed unsurpassed credibility with all of his colleagues.

The story of Senator Sarbanes' father, Spyros, and the president of Princeton University shows other aspects of *philotimo*—pride and humility, gratitude, and generosity. Sarbanes' father, a modestly educated immigrant from Greece, owned the small Mayflower Grill restaurant in Salisbury, Maryland, a town then of 15,000. At Sarbanes' graduation from Princeton, he was shocked to see the president of Princeton treating his father as though they knew each other.

Sarbanes later learned that his parents, overwhelmed that their son was able to attend the university frequently considered the best in America and the world, were driven by their *philotimo* to do something very unusual. When they visited Sarbanes at Princeton, they would always bring a cooked roast from their restaurant to the back-kitchen door of the Princeton president's house. Over the years, Sarbanes' father and the school's president came to know and appreciate each other. Only pride, appreciation, humility, and generosity would formulate such conduct.

Philotimo may also explain why Greek Americans have such a high percentage of personal friends who are also Greek American. Showing *philotimo* and sacrificing for a Greek American friend in the community is more likely to produce reciprocal love and respect because Greeks have been brought up, consciously or subconsciously, realizing that appreciation and indebtedness is an appropriate part of *philotimo*. This is evident in many ways, both apparent and subtle. For example, if one has a fellow Greek taking care of his home air conditioning system and it breaks down on a holiday, a Greek repairman's *philotimo* will likely inspire him to fix the appliance, even in the middle of a holiday and at no extra charge.

I have seen numerous cases where this can be of lifesaving importance. In one case, an individual who had a doctor remove a malignancy felt another similar growth and his doctor could not see him for two weeks. Rather than wait, he contacted a Greek American doctor whom he had never met but knew people who knew her. She fit him in within hours of his call.

Consider realtor Leon Andris. For his *koumbari* and close friends who were purchasing a home, he routinely offered to do their broker work without charging them the three percent of the sales price that usually went to the broker. Most homes in his area of Montgomery County, Maryland, sell for over $1 million, meaning that he saved many friends over $30,000. Over time it amounted to a lot of money just among those of whom I am aware.

The most far-reaching, multifaceted practice of *philotimo* we have seen is that of the aforementioned Father Karloutsos. Having worked closely with Father for 50 years, I can attest that virtually every day in addition to helping the Ecumenical Patriarchate, the Archdiocese, and the Orthodox faithful with their faith and with life and death matters, he also goes out of his way with more secular issues. It might involve helping a child's college aspirations, securing employment for someone, overcoming a major governmental issue or anything else by using his extraordinary network of people who can provide for those who need the help.

The *philotimo* of the Hellenes who felt compelled to reciprocate to Father included the over 1,300 people who attended what was, in effect, a thank you dinner in his honor, as well as his wife's, in 2018. The $1 million proceeds from that dinner event went toward support for the Ecumenical Patriarchate. Among the huge number in attendance were grateful Orthodox Christians whose contributions made up a major part of his career's fundraising efforts for the church, exceeding one-third of a billion dollars. His *philotimo* was also recognized by the President of the United States who presented him with the Presidential Medal of Freedom.

More *philotimo* in action: when a Greek American visiting Greece bought lunch for his group of friends at a small, local restaurant, he happened to tell the restaurant owner that he loved the design on his coffee cups. When he left, the owner presented the fellow who complimented the design with a box of those coffee cups to keep.

Another aspect of *philotimo* is called *philoxenia* (*philos*, meaning friend of or love of and *xenia*, meaning stranger)—friend of the stranger. This is the reason why many non-Greeks visiting Greece frequently describe the Greek people as extraordinarily friendly and helpful.

Agnos, the Greek American mayor of one of America's premier cities, San Francisco, California, recalled the following. While he was running for mayor, he went around the country raising funds for his election campaign. He said, "Wherever I went, Greek Americans generously supported me. They did it for one reason: *philotimo*."

Such trust among Hellenes in America is of particular value at this moment in US history. According to David Brooks, a major American thought leader, "In America, interpersonal trust is in catastrophic decline." In 2014 according to the General Social Survey conducted by the National Opinion Research Center at the University of Chicago, only 30.3 percent of Americans agreed that "most people can be trusted," the lowest number the survey has recorded since it started asking the question in 1972. Today, a majority of Americans say they don't trust other people when they first meet them. Gratefully, that is not the situation for Hellenic Americans meeting each other.

A very young man who was starting a company knew he needed people he could trust. He went to his Greek Orthodox priest instead of some management consultant. Before he knew it, at the rec-ommendation of the priest, he had a substantial staff and they were all Greek. He knew that each of these people he hired had a lot riding on their reputation as top employees. To be considered otherwise would have been a blot on their *philotimo* by the people most important to their lives, their grandparents, parents, uncles, aunts, and the priest himself.

There are a few Hellenes who through *philotimo* have achieved the virtually impossible in today's competitive world. They sail through life's challenges, rising beyond their peers without causing even one person to develop a negative feeling toward them. I have happily encountered many who well might qualify. But three I have seen as closely as would their valet if they had one—and they say that "no man is a hero to his valet." My Uncle George Manatos of Wyoming and California, Tony Kaculis of the Washington, DC area, and my koumbaro Stratton Liapis of Washington, DC, have somehow accomplished this wonderful feat.

A short video that explains this powerful concept of *philotimo* has been viewed over one million times online and elsewhere. College professors have used this video in their modern Greek studies programs as well as other classes. This *philotimo* video speaks to those involved in many different degrees of Hellenism.

It inspired a Hellenic ICU physician fighting COVID-19 on the front lines in Melbourne, Australia, who recently saw the *philotimo* Greek Secret video online. He wrote to us,

> *Your video has given me strength during these difficult times. ... Our door (here in Melbourne) is always open for you, your family, or any of the other Greek Americans who have helped you produce the video.*

It describes so well the magic in Hellenism, it is worth repeating the link to that video— https://www.oxidayfoundation.org/philotimo/the-greek-secret/

During the follow-up to the 2020 presidential election, two Hellenic federal judges of the 3rd Circuit Court of Appeals made national news by showing their *philotimo,* their love of honor. They were Stephanos Bibas, appointed by President Trump, and Michael Chagares, appointed by President Bush. These displays of *philotimo* occurred in the midst of an unusual cynical national atmosphere. Some serious people believed that Republican-appointed federal judges might deemphasize their judicial neutrality and find in favor of President Trump's request to throw out one million votes in Pennsylvania. Proudly, Hellenes were not surprised when Judge Bibas and Judge Chagares showed their *philotimo* and judicial wisdom and rejected the appeal.

CHAPTER 3

Greek Characteristics That Surpass Most Nationalities

Familial Relationships—Greeks and Greek Americans see each other as family

The familial feeling among Greeks can be seen in day-to-day life. For example, some Greek Americans stay seated at the end of every movie as the credits roll and scour the names to see if a Greek name is listed or a Greek is involved in the movie in any way. As Governor and US Democratic nominee for the presidency in 1988, Mike Dukakis said,

> *If I see a Greek somewhere in the country was appointed to an important position, it makes me feel good.*

During Dukakis' campaign for president, the base of his financial backing was the Greek American community. Amazingly, this enabled him to raise more primary election campaign funds than any other candidate in history from either political party at that time. Many of those contributions came from Republican Greek Americans who disagreed with nearly all his policies. But the idea of having a "Greek Boy," as the Greeks affectionately referred to any fellow Greek male, in the White House was more important to them.

If a Greek American overhears that someone else has a Greek name, he or she will likely approach the person to see what part of Greece their family is from and whom they know in common. It was not uncommon in the 1980s for Greek Americans to encounter *philotimo* from other Hellenes on trips with their children such as restaurant owners giving candy bars from a display case to the children of these newly acquainted Greek Americans. Today it's not unusual to get a free dessert. That's familial *philotimo*.

Another aspect of the familial nature of Hellenism aligns similarly with a benefit of graduating from Princeton, Harvard, Yale, or other top universities—a school club in major cities. Graduates of these schools have a place where they can find a group of intelligent and successful people who have all had a common experience and who will probably treat them well. The Greek Orthodox Church functions similarly for Greeks. When Greeks go to church, they encounter virtually only Greeks or others who have married Greeks, unlike Catholics and other religions who find people of many national origins at church on Sundays. Like the graduates of those top schools, members of the Greek Orthodox Church community will generally be bright, successful, and interested in learning about you. Once you become known, you will certainly be treated with warmth and generosity.

The familial feeling among Hellenes enables them to automatically experience the warmth of small-town living within large urban areas. The lament that people feel lonely even though they are surrounded by millions in a big city does not readily apply to Hellenes. Every big city in America has a community with whom Hellenes can easily resonate—other Hellenes. There is a strikingly similar worldview among Hellenes regardless of where they live.

A college-age Greek American student attending a Greek Orthodox Church in a new city in the mid-1900s would invariably have some Greek woman ask where he or she was from and strike up a con-versation. More often than not, that woman would then ask the student to her home for Sunday lunch with her family. Part of that invitation was based on her *philotimo* and part on her subconscious matchmaking inclination for her own child or a relative.

This familial Hellenic feeling can also be profitable. A young Greek American woman moved from one investment bank to another and her name was listed with her new bank. Her first customers whom she did not know were all Greeks. They saw her name, met her, and moved their accounts to under her control. As in so many other situations, these Greeks realized that she would likely be more trustworthy than a stranger. They also knew that whether conscious or not, there was a great likelihood that *philotimo* played a role in her value system.

The familial Greek aspect of taking care of each other was also reflected in a humorous video by Greek American actress and comedian Alyssa Limperis. It played on the pride Greeks and Greek Americans felt when one of the vaccines found to stop the world-wide, mass-killing COVID-19 was developed by a Greek—Albert Bourla. He is the CEO of Pfizer, and he grew up in the Greek Jewish community in Thessaloniki, Greece.

Pretending to be an old, thick Greek-accented, Greek grandmother (*yiayia*) who was having a difficult time with the English language, Limperis spoke about Bourla and his vaccine. Limperis said, "You hear the CEO of Pfizer is Greek. Yes, the Pfizer vaccine the big strong one, the best one of course it's from Greece. Moderna no, no take the Moderna. I no trust the Moderna. Pfizer oh yes, Greek Boy make Pfizer very good. Very good boy. They say to get it twice. No, going in, you say you Greek. They give it to you six or seven times." Her humor reflected how Greeks tend to take care of each other.

Relatives of Choice—Greeks select those with whom they want a family relationship

The saying, "You can pick your friends but not your relatives" is not so true in the Greek tradition because one can choose their *koumbari* who become like a first cousin. *Koumbari* are people who serve as the best man or maid of honor at your wedding, or a godparent of one of your children, or a person for whom you were a best man or maid of honor or for whom you are a godparent to a child. Other cultures have similar relationships.

Typically, a *koumbari* gets the benefits a Hellene with *philotimo* would give to a first cousin. For example, if asked by a first cousin to borrow $10,000 or $20,000 "no questions asked," a first cousin with *philotimo* would probably loan the money. Part of the reason this happens is because it is understood that the person receiving the loan would not spend a dollar on anything beyond necessities before paying back the loan.

Typically, *koumbari* make up a high percentage of a Greek's life-long social circle. In one of many anecdotal examples, a group of six male *koumbari* over the age of 70 meet for dinner every other Monday evening. They enjoy it for a number of reasons, including the support they provide for each other as well as the opportunity to share stories and jokes that they enjoyed together nearly half a century earlier.

Sacrifices for Progeny—Greek immigrants in the western US suffered but provided a mutual safety net and cherished the future opportunities for their children

The Greeks who came to America in the early 1900s were, as mentioned previously, so universally poor and lacking formal education that in order to secure food, they were forced to take the most menial and dangerous jobs that, at the time, most Americans would not take. The overwhelming majority of the first Greeks who came over from Greece were male. As mentioned, most intended to make a fortune and return home, but instead only about 30 percent actually did. Many of the men had their travel from Greece paid for by a "padrone," a labor boss who, in exchange, retained a percentage of their paychecks, some for many years. The vast majority of such padrones secured dangerous jobs in the mines in the western United States. Because of this system, in 1920 a majority of Greek immigrants lived west of the Mississippi River.

Years after these first male waves of Greek immigrants came to America, many married women who were nearly exclusively in or from Greece and began families. In the town of Rock Springs, Wyoming, for example, there were 100 Greek families in 1920. An analysis of coal mine records there showed that typically 30 heads of Greek American households died in mine cave-ins over a typical 20-year period. That fatality rate is far higher than soldiers experience in most wars.

GREECE IN N.Y. 4TH JULY PARADE

These shocking numbers do not include the many Greek American miners who were not killed, but who suffered from black lung disease, impeding their breathing and significantly shortening their lives. The difficulty of this work can also be more easily understood by the realization that many of these miners saw the sun only on weekends. In the winter, they went into the mine before the sun came up, ate lunch amid the coal dust, and emerged from the mine long after the sun had set.

Life was very tough. Typically, the miners lived in small houses, many owned by the coal mine company. The walls of the houses had no insulation, some bathrooms were outhouses, in some coal camps the only showers were communal up the street at the coal mine facility, and the only heat in these homes typically came from a coal stove in the kitchen. This life was particularly hard in Rock Springs where the average temperatures in December and January were a low of 13°F (-10°C) and a high just below freezing 30°F (-1°C). And these temperatures were exacerbated in Wyoming, America's windiest state, with winter wind gusts exceeding 50 mph.

In virtually every case, miners' wives spoke English poorly since they interacted nearly exclusively with other Greeks, and their children were typically three to five in number. Two days after a miner was killed, his family would be kicked out of their home owned by the mining company. Luckily, the built-in safety net of their Hellenism meant that virtually every one of the wives and children of these Greeks who perished in the mines found significant help from relatives, *koumbari*, people who came from their village in Greece, and other Greek friends. The safety net and their *philotimo* assured that no one starved and nearly all had good lives despite the tragedy.

In Utah, the Sargetakis family's head of household died in the mine and left a wife and four young sons—little Ted, John, Steve, and Mike. Unable to make enough to feed her children, the mother found close Hellenes living in other coal towns within 100 miles. Each took in one of the children and raised them as one of their own. The four young, terrified boys vowed to reunite when they grew up and go into business together. They did just that and created Silver State Fabrics, which became the biggest fabric company in Utah.

These first Greek Americans out west also encountered tremendous discrimination. In Price, Utah, for example, according to the renowned Greek American author, Harry Mark Petrakis, stores had signs in the window that read, "WE ARE 100% AMERICAN" and even "NO N_____S OR GREEKS." The *New York Times* reported that 3,000 men in Omaha, Nebraska, attacked a Greek neighborhood from which the subsequent Greek American Secretary of Commerce in the Nixon Administration, Pete Peterson, arose. The mob looted Greek businesses and homes, beating Greek men, women, and children. In the state of Georgia, it was the attacks of the Ku Klux Klan against Greeks that led to the creation of Greek Americans' largest fraternal organization, AHEPA.

Although their lives and high number of deaths would be considered by many to be hell, the *philotimo* of these Greek immigrants enabled them to see the circumstances differently. They were extremely grateful to be Americans. In their minds, the thought that they were free from the horrors of 400 years of Ottoman occupation, had free educations for all their children, and had a chance at prosperity brought unimaginable fulfillment to their lives. There were no prouder Americans.

Many years later, during the 1980s, some teenage Greek American boys criticized America in the presence of one of those early Greek immigrants. His reaction was typical. He approached them and, in his very thick Greek accent, sternly told them as he pointed to the ground, "You should fall on your knees and thank God you live in America."

All the early Greek immigrants experienced a difficult time in the United States. Nowhere were they welcomed with open arms. However, those in the western US may have received the most difficult treatment. Their degree of suffering was not universal. That immigrant suffering and sacrifice, primarily for their progeny, moved their children, grandchildren. and even great grandchildren to feel an extremely deep debt of gratitude and obligation toward them.

This profound feeling of indebtedness by some Greek Americans, as for many Americans, was given voice in the famous film, *Saving Private Ryan*. The movie detailed how a number of Ryan's fellow soldiers and friends gave their lives to save his. Many Greek Americans shared the tears shed by Private Ryan who said as an old man looking back,

I lived my life the best I could, and I hope that in your eyes it is enough to have earned what all of you have done for me.

The laws and regulations regarding Greek immigration to America changed over the years. The big immigration around 1910 required the person immigrating to have identified someone in America who could vouch for him. Frequently, they were additionally required to identify how they would make a living. Most in that mass migration arrived legally.

However, over the years, some arrived illegally, especially between 1924 and 1965 when the "Golden Door" of immigration at least partially closed. Some Greeks used rather crafty methods. One fellow, John Manolatos, a soft-spoken young man who came on a Greek ship in the 1930s, used a push broom to sweep the gangplank from which the legal immigrants disembarked to meet the US immigration officials. He then swept the shore area in front of, around, and behind the immigration officials—and into America. He later married a Greek American woman and secured his US citizenship. The level of intelligence that created that unique arrival must have been passed on to his son Telemachos (Telly) who went on to receive his graduate degree in electrical engineering at Stanford University.

Another interesting Greek arrival story took place in Denver years after the mass immigration. This particular Greek raised a family and established a number of hamburger restaurants and other stores. Then, immigration officials arrived at one of his hamburger restaurants one day around lunchtime. Instead of arresting him, they adhered to his request to come back after the lunch rush was over. In the end, in light of his contributions to the American economy, they enabled him to become a US citizen. One of his sons went on to become a lawyer and then a judge in Colorado.

Restaurants certainly played a major role in the success of the Greeks in America. Not very many years after these Greek immigrants arrived, you nearly couldn't find a city or town that didn't have a Greek restaurant. They so much wanted to be seen as Americans that many chose very deeply American names for their restaurants, like the Mayflower. In the 1950s and 1960s, if you saw a restaurant with such a name it was nearly always Greek owned and operated.

Even today Greek Americans across the country are still deeply involved in the restaurant business. It is so much a part of Greeks that it struck even one of the Greek Americans who is worth billions of dollars from his field of commercial real estate, George Marcus of Palo Alto, California. Amid his seemingly 24-hour-a-day focus on commercial real estate, he found time to open a Greek restaurant in San Francisco and in Palo Alto—Kokkari Estiatorio (selected by Zagat as #1 in region) and Evvia Estiatorio, respectively.

Extraordinary Health and Longevity—The ancient Greeks created modern medicine and modern Greeks popularized one of the world's healthiest lifestyles

Hippocrates, of Classical Greece, who is commonly referred to as "The Father of Western Medicine," is well known for his Hippocratic Oath that modern doctors take upon entering the profession today. And, many of the modern world's top doctors have Greek backgrounds. Dr. George Papanikolaou (originally from Kos), for example, invented the "Pap test" that detects cervical cancer and Dr. George Cotzias (originally from Crete, Greece) invented L-Dopa, a major breakthrough medicine in the treatment of Parkinson's disease. One of the most respected doctors who retired from the world's foremost medical research center, the National Institutes of Health, is Dr. Nicholas Patronas. His *philotimo* has moved him to give his nationally renowned reputation and medical expertise to improve the health of hundreds of Hellenes, at no charge. He also saved the lives of over a hundred I am aware of who asked him for help. He did the same for some non-Hellenes as well.

And, America is covered with Hellenic doctors beloved by their patients and their grateful *koumbari* who have gotten hundreds of thousands of dollars' worth of free medical advice. They are like Washington, DC's pediatrician Dr. Michael Datch ("Detsis" until an Ellis Island official couldn't understand his father's Greek accent and declared his name to be Datch) who was worshipped by many Greek American mothers who entrusted their children's lives to him.

Whatever force moved Hippocrates to somehow find life-improving and lifesaving foods and practices that others could not find remains alive in the Greek people. This is particularly true with respect to heart attacks. In the 1960s, a seven-nation study ranging from Finland to the United States to Japan was undertaken to compare coronary artery disease in 13,000 men aged 40 to 59. The study found that Cretan residents had the lowest rate of coronary vascular disease of all the populations observed ("The Cretan Diet," *Today's Dietician*, 2007). A major finding of the study was that the premature death rate from heart attack for Greek/Cretan men was 90 percent lower than that of American men. A follow-up of that study in 1991 found that all 700 men studied in Finland had died whereas of all the men studied in Crete, Greece, only half had passed away. Greeks have found ways to live that enable them to be among the healthiest in the world.

Additionally, an analysis of premature death rates from all diseases some years ago found that the Greek people compare extremely well to the rest of the world population. With the exception of some types of cancers, Greek people rank among the top 10 percent with the least fatalities from all other diseases. Like the other momentous Greek accomplishments, this did not happen by chance.

Many old Greek immigrants had their own kind of unique, village-type health practices which frequently embarrassed their Americanized children. In the 1950s, it was not unheard of to see an old Greek woman on her hands and knees, digging up dandelion greens in a public park. It was a fairly common practice among these women. Even more out of step with America in those days and embarrassing to their children was the seemingly useless *vendouzes*—treating an ill person by heating the inside of a cup and pressing it to the skin of a sick person so that the flesh was sucked into the cup.

As was the case with so many seemingly foolish village practices, as America and the world's medical science progressed, the wisdom of those practices was validated. In 2016 the greatest Olympic gold medal winner of all time, Michael Phelps, had purple circles covering much of his body—you guessed it, the result of *vendouzes*. And today one of America's most highly regarded medical centers, the Cleveland Clinic, reported in July of 2021, "Dandelions pack a whole lot of vitamins and minerals into a small plant … they are probably the most nutritiously dense green you can eat—outstripping even kale or spinach. Dandelion greens, in particular, are a great source of vitamins and minerals such as Vitamin A, C, and K." Those old-timers knew what they were doing.

These two somewhat comical examples are indicative of how over the centuries, Greeks spontaneously developed a lifestyle—diet, exercise, social activity, etc.—that clearly promoted longer life expectancy. And, again, it is not by chance that a Greek American woman, Dr. Artemis Simopoulos, discovered the crucial importance of what is now widely known as the Mediterranean Diet. In the 1970s, Dr. Simopoulos was at the National Institutes of Health when she discovered that the Omega 3 fatty acids were "the magic" elements in the foods of Crete that dramatically prolonged life. The Cretans consumed the Omega 3 fatty acids primarily in large amounts of olive oil, fish, and even in properly grazed animals. Her discoveries brought life-extending information to hundreds of millions of people around the world.

Alzheimer's and Alcoholism

Greeks in America as compared to other nationalities have shown very well with respect to Alzheimer's/dementia. It was not unusual for a Greek American to grow up seeing only one older Greek American with dementia while seeing many with it among older people in the families of his or her non-Greek friends. According to data from the world's and America's top health organizations, America ranks 44th in the world with respect to our incidence of death from Alzheimer's/dementia with 32.4 per 100,000 Americans. Greece, however, ranks 155th with only 5.6 per 100,000 Greeks.

The same can be said about Greeks and alcoholism. Growing up Greek American, one sees wine consumed very readily at most

Greek events, but a drunk Hellene is virtually never seen. According to World Life Expectancy, data from the top health organizations rank America 50th with 2.6 deaths from alcoholism per 100,000 Americans and Greece at 178th with only .2 deaths per 100,000 Greeks.

Orthodox Faith and Philosophy

The Greek Orthodox Church plays a large role in the life and *philotimo* of typical Greek Americans and in the life of Greeks around the world. Greek Orthodoxy provides Hellenes effective grounding and comfort. It instructs them how to lead a moral and compassionate life.

The spiritual head of all Orthodox Christians, Ecumenical Patriarch Bartholomew, is the 269th direct successor of the first

His All-Holiness Ecumenical Patriarch Bartholomew

His Eminence Archbishop Elpidophoros

Apostle—Andrew. A learned Hellene who speaks eight languages, the Patriarch was, as mentioned earlier, chosen to be one of the few people, like Washington and Churchill, to receive the Congressional Gold Medal. To Orthodox Christians, it is inspiring that he was the first international environmentalist chosen by the United Nations as a Laureate Champion of the Earth and also the first religious leader to move Muslim leaders to condemn as non-religious acts the 9/11 attacks on America.

Also, with respect to His All-Holiness the Ecumenical Patriarch, President Biden, who in his time in the US Senate and as Vice President had met virtually every leader in the world, said around 2010,

*As a practicing Catholic I must say that the two most
Christ-like people I have met in the world are Nelson
Mandela and Ecumenical Patriarch Bartholomew.*

No wonder this is so. The theology of the Greek Orthodox Church
is primarily based on love of God and of our fellow human beings.
This theology contributes greatly to Hellenic principles, like *philotimo,* that direct the lives of so many Greeks. Further, it is no
coincidence that the leaders of Greece's anti-Holocaust efforts were
the backbone of the Greek Orthodox faith—the archbishop, metro-
politans, bishops, priests, monks, and even nuns (including Queen
Elizabeth's mother-in-law). Unlike some faiths that badly failed the
ultimate test during Hitler and the Holocaust, the Orthodox Church
leaders resisted Hitler and the Axis Forces. The church's devotion to
those marked for extermination was truly unsurpassed.

Unlike some other faiths in America, Greek Orthodoxy emphasizes
the mystery of faith and God. It is far more accepting of those who
agree with Aristotle's well-known quotation of Socrates, *"I know
that I know nothing."* The church's acceptance of the mystery of
God might make it easier for Orthodox to be more comfortable
with the latest surprising scientific breakthroughs than other faiths
that have a more literal interpretation of scripture or that dictate
church positions with rigid certainty. It can handle, for example,
the new discovery in quantum physics that particles, upon which
all material things are made, are only particles when observed and
when unobserved they become waves. At least in the quantum
world, what we see is not what is.

The Greek Orthodox Church is in line with our Hellenic culture
and its rich philosophical tradition. Indeed, most Hellenes know
some of what the sages of ancient Greece taught us. One example is
the quote, *"Everything in moderation."* Even though this adage was
first expressed in the 6th century BC, it is taught to many Greeks
today. The famous modern Greek writer, Nikos Kazantzakis, the
author of *Zorba the Greek* and many other successful books, even
had his own version of religion to which some Greeks can relate.

He said,

*God changes appearances every second. Blessed is the man
who can recognize him in all his disguises. One moment
he is a glass of fresh water, the next your son bouncing on
your knees or an enchanting woman, or perhaps merely a
morning walk.*

Although many of the early immigrating Greek Americans lacked
formal education, virtually all of them had the equivalent of a PhD in
what we call "village wisdom." Virtually every Greek has learned this
wisdom from fathers and mothers, uncles, aunts, and grandparents.
Years ago, a poorly educated Greek American grandfather told his
grandson, "If you spend a day and night with blind people when
you wake up the next morning you too will not be able to see." The
American expression with the same wisdom is "Show me your friends
and I will show you who you are." The *yiayias* (grandmothers) and
papous (grandfathers) in America, even without formal education,
knew what to do and what not to do in order to have a "good life."

Further proof of the value of Hellenic wisdom involves one of the
most privileged, well-educated and highly regarded US presidents of
the modern era, John F. Kennedy. He was a man who had access to
virtually everything that is conventionally thought of as producing
happiness—a large circle of family and friends, great wealth, great
power, world-wide fame, a beautiful and brilliant wife, wonderful
children, good looks, athletic ability, intelligence, and a great sense
of humor. Yet, when he was asked the question, in a 1963 press
conference, "What brings you the greatest pleasure," he did not
answer with any of his assets mentioned above. Instead, he replied,

*The Greeks were right when they said, Happiness is the full
use of your powers along lines of excellence.*

He was referring to Hellenism and the benefits that spring
therefrom.

Orthodoxy and Dignity

The Greek people put a premium on dignity. It might be best seen in the following imagined scenario. One could take from Greece a poor and marginally educated person, and if you bought him a shirt, tie, and suit and gave him a shave, you could bring him to a White House reception, and by his conduct, he would be hard to distinguish from the other attendees.

An Ethiopian American was asked if the same could be said about Ethiopians. He went on to say that yes and this was because of the two nationalities' common religion of Orthodox Christianity.

It was the opinion of this Ethiopian American that Orthodoxy, as compared to many other religions including other denominations of Christianity, takes the concepts of humility, respect, and contained conduct to a higher level of focus. One example to support his contention is that Orthodoxy is one of the very few religions in America where the parishioners routinely kiss the hand of the priest. It is a faith steeped in tradition and humility. He said that even the least sophisticated Greek or Ethiopian would respect the surroundings and would not think of taking it upon him or herself to impolitely contest anything that was said in a setting such as the White House.

Growing up Greek American in the 20th century left another strong impression regarding familial civility. The television programs and songs of the late 1950s and 1960s portrayed households of peace and cooperation, aside from slight course corrections needed by all children everywhere. The families portrayed in the television programs of *Father Knows Best* and *Leave It to Beaver*, for example, made family life look idyllic and non-dysfunctional.

However, beginning in the late 1960s and the 1970s, large numbers of people attacked those portrayals as false and unrealistic—hiding the actual "dysfunctional" households that were indicated to be the norm. Discussions about these contrasting descriptions of American households revealed an interesting cultural distinction. Those Greek American households one got a deep look into—one's own, one's aunt and uncle, one's grandparents, one's Sunday School classmates as well as one's Hellenic classmates at school—were found by virtually all the Hellenes of that era to have been very similar to the *Leave It to Beaver* portrayals. The only real differences with the television portrayals were the Mediterranean practice of speaking with exasperation or yelling and other idiosyncratic ethnocentric behaviors that were well depicted in the film *My Big Fat Greek Wedding*. But the resulting civility and harmony were very similar.

For whatever reason, probably not wanting to disappoint or embarrass parents, grandparents, uncles and aunts or besmirch a family history of upstanding conduct and respect, Greek American households of that era were quite civilized. Stories of domestic violence, with the exception of frequent spankings but only on the rear end, were unheard of in Greek American households of that era and today. Interestingly, discussions with Jewish, Asian, and some other friends of that era found the very same analysis as that of the Greeks.

Hospitality and Food

Greeks use food as a demonstration of caring and bonding, a measure of a household's honor, and for many other purposes. This is apparent in the relatively high percentage of Greeks in the restaurant business, as well as in other ways. In the years of the very poor Greek immigrants, it was not unusual for types of food, usually equated with significant wealth, to be put out for guests. I will never forget being at a dinner in 1954, seeing a presentation of food including three different types of meat, among many other things. It was set out in the 12' × 12' living room of a blind retired coal miner and his wife who were barely scraping by.

Greek American focus on food was also evident at a White House celebration event in 1978 that included all 535 US senators and members of Congress and their families—it must have included 1,500 to 2,000 people. When my wife and I entered, I kiddingly said to her, "Let's go by the food table to see if Congressmen Sarbanes and Brademas (both Greek Americans) are here." Believe it or not, there they were, as I had suspected, enjoying the food. As well, whenever a Hellene is entertaining non-Greeks, the rule is some liquor and food. But when the guests are Greeks, the rule is much less liquor and a great deal of food.

And, this extravagance of food in Greek American households is nothing compared to the tradition in Greece. When visiting relatives in Greece, going from one village to another, frequently we would sit down at one second or third cousin's home for a great lunch at noon and leave for the next village at 1:30 p.m. Our relatives hosting us in the next village would, upon arrival, serve us nice drinks. The hostess would then disappear into the kitchen and no amount of explanation that we were full because we just finished lunch would stop her. At around 2:00 p.m., she would emerge with a full meal. And, surprisingly to our Greek American minds, if we did not eat a significant second meal at her house, she would be seriously offended. So, we would, with difficulty, gratefully enjoy another great meal.

CHAPTER 4

Why Greeks Are Able to Achieve So Much

Did the Ottoman Occupation Sharpen Greek Wits?

Some have suggested that some of these Greek characteristics may have emerged because of 400 years of Ottoman
occupation of Greece. They propose that, like the Jewish
community that has lived in many locales under persecution
for centuries, one's wits are sharpened. Churchill noticed
similarities between the Greeks and the Jews,

> *Both (Greeks and Jews) have shown the capacity for*
> *survival, in spite of unending perils and suffering*
> *from external oppressors. They have survived*
> *in spite of all the world could do against them.*
> *Personally, I have been on the side of both and*
> *believed in their invincible power to survive ... the*
> *world tides threatening their extinction.*

In Homer's epic poem, the *Iliad*, he describes Greek characteristics that enabled Hellenes to withstand adversity. The
story's hero, Odysseus, owes his greatness to intellect, guile,
and versatility. He describes Odysseus as brave, loyal, smart,
wise, strong, shrewd, cunning, and majestic.

These abilities enabled Odysseus to uniquely put an end
to the 10-year siege of Troy with the famous deception of
the "Trojan Horse." While pretending to burn their tents

and retreat, Odysseus left only a huge wooden horse they had built, hidden inside of which were a few dozen of the best of the Greek soldiers. When night fell, they escaped the horse and opened the gates of Troy, thus enabling a Greek victory to end the 10-year-old war.

Homer's message regarding the most valuable of Greek abilities seems to point to a particular cleverness. This seems to enable clearheaded assessment of the circumstance, an inventiveness to find solutions "out of the box" and the courage, cunning, and versatility to effectively implement the winning strategy.

The harsh Ottoman control over some parts of Greece (and Macedonia, Epirus, and Crete) persisted until 1913, when the empire lost the Balkan Wars. Being most familiar with the harsh treatment of the Cretan Greeks that continued into the late 1800s, I will limit my focus there. Part of the reason for this treatment could have resulted from the fact that Crete was a particularly rebellious place. Years ago, a listing of the uprisings that took place in Crete led me to conclude that they occurred, on average, once every seven years.

Harsh treatment by the Turks in Crete extending into the very late 1800s is one of the reasons given for why the women of Crete were so uniquely adept at killing Nazi paratrooper invaders in WWII. A quote from one of the Cretan women, on her way out the door to take on the Nazi paratroopers, supports this contention: "Here we go again."

The Ottoman occupation of Crete certainly qualifies in terms of the horrors that the Greeks experienced. The writings of Kazantzakis, who lived during my lifetime, from 1883 to 1957, details these terrible conditions. He tells of his somewhat common experience in Crete involving a band of Turks moving through his Cretan village. He explains how, when this occurred, his father would barricade his mother, his sister, and him behind the locked front door of their small home. They listened to, in his words, *"the frenzied Turks in the street outside, cursing, threatening, breaking down doors and slaughtering Christians. We heard dogs barking, the cries and death rales of the wounded, and a droning in the air as though an earthquake was in progress."* As they listened, his father carried his loaded musket in his belt as he sharpened his large black handled knife on an oblong whetstone. He told his family that if the Turks were to break in their door he would quickly kill them to save them from *"falling into the Turks' hands."*

During the 1700s and early 1800s of that occupation, Greek children were taken, effectively into slavery, by the Ottomans and the Barbers. Although the number of slaves the North African Barbers took from Europe, as far north as Ireland, is unclear, it surpassed the number of slaves brought to what is today America.

The aforementioned Adondakis family has a story of such slavery. A very young Adondakis boy was abducted from the city of Chania, Crete. Many years later, as a very young man he escaped and went back to Chania. He was so young when taken he could remember little other than sitting on a prominent rock in Chania, which he immediately sat on again upon his return. Amazingly, his mother happened to walk past that rock where she had last seen him as a child. She recognized her son and her dream and his came true.

Could Greeks' inclination to show courage today also have something to do with stories about those who did not show courage during the Ottoman occupation? Answering the question of why he showed such bravery, one young boy living in Crete during the Nazi invasion said, "I remember how badly those who did not show courage during the Ottoman occupation were thought of forever."

Raised to Be Their Best—Is it the way the Greeks are born or brought up?

Others wonder if the Greek strive for excellence results from virtually every young Greek child being told of the greatness of the Ancient Greeks. Could this cause a Greek child to feel that greatness was possible even if they were poor?

Greek Americans never lacked confidence. Some of that attitude clearly had to do with the Golden Age. An example of Greek confidence in Hellenism was an expression that numerous Greek Americans used among themselves in the 1950s regarding other Americans looking down on them.

An 11-year-old Greek American boy innocently and embarrassingly used this expression thinking it was simply a statement of fact. When a wealthy American, non-Greek, woman asked him if discrimination had caused him to feel lesser than other Americans, he answered, *"No, because our ancestors were writing in books while yours were still swinging in trees."* No bigoted meaning was intended but the look on the woman's face made him realize that outside his home that may not be the most appropriate thing to say.

The supreme confidence of the Greek people may be the result of their subconscious belief in their natural abilities compared to those of others. Or it could be the extraordinary amount of attention and praise Hellenes universally receive from their parents and family from the moment they are born. With such constant encouragement, children's slightest achievements might serve as the secret formula enabling Greeks to accomplish so much.

Or it could have something to do with inclinations determined by inherited DNA. Scandinavian studies of thousands of adopted children in the 1980s and '90s found that the criminal record of the adopted children was closer to that of the biological parents than the adoptive parents. According to the National Institutes of Health, adopted children of a biological parent with criminal behavior had elevated criminal records.

An anecdotal story covering over two decades also suggests a possibility of some influence of inherited traits. Over that 25-year period, every time a person with a Greek last name was charged with a murder in the metropolitan area of Washington, DC, this Greek American woman would say, "I'll bet he is not all Greek," meaning that his mother probably has no Greek blood. She was thought to be prejudiced for her ethnicity, but in such cases, over all those years a follow-up inquiry found her to be correct an overwhelming percent of the time. There are numerous other anecdotal stories covering different subjects that also show the same result. It's not that Greeks don't do bad things; it is just that they don't do nearly as many nor as bad.

CHAPTER 5

Somewhat Unique Hellenic Traits

What follows is derived primarily from observation of one part of the Greek American community for over half a century.

Not Easily Led

Some cultural contrasts between the Greek Americans and what were referred to as "regular Americans" revealed themselves in a survey of 25 non-Greeks and 25 Greek Americans taken three decades ago. The answers to two questions differed most strikingly. One question was added to the survey to reveal some truth and some humor. It exposed a quality that many Greeks will recognize. Only 20 percent of the non-Greeks answered yes to this question in comparison with 80 percent of the Greek Americans. The question asked, "Does this statement describe the belief of people of your ethnic background? 'I see things a little more clearly than everyone else and I should really be in charge of everything.'" The telling of this result always evokes a very big laugh from Greek Americans. They seem to recognize the accuracy and comedy of the observation and its self-confidence.

The contrast between the self-confidence of Hellenes compared to non-Hellenes shows up in many different ways in America. A Greek American attended a conference made up of about 25 vice presidents of major American corporations and their spouses. A professor from a leading university was heading the conference and made an effective presentation in which he proposed that with goal setting and intensive focus, one can accomplish anything they wish to achieve. He emphasized that there is no limit to this approach. The group as a whole accepted his thesis; however, one participant challenged the statement.

A Greek American in the audience posed a question to the professor. He said that while he agreed with the general thesis, he wanted to set the world record for the 100-meter sprint at the next Olympics and that was impossible regardless of his goal setting and focus. One other person was skeptical of the professor's thesis. Soon thereafter that discussion stopped with a break for refreshments. The Greek American who posed the sprint question spoke to the other skeptic at the conference who, of course, turned out to also be Greek.

This Hellenic inability to be easily led by authority figures that are demanding showed up once more at the Kennedy Center for the Performing Arts in Washington, DC. At an event for then President Reagan, the video producer of the performance that was going to later be nationally televised told the audience from the stage that he wanted to shoot audience cutaways before the president arrived and the event began. He asked the audience to applaud at his command. After the audience's applause, he expressed great disappointment in how weak it was and said, somewhat harshly, that at his next command they should applaud more vigorously. The audience eagerly complied and applauded with vigor at his next command.

Next, the television producer said that he was sure the audience would want to give this event a standing ovation at some point. He then added that at his next command the audience should enthusiastically give a standing ovation. A little voice in the Greek American's head said to himself, "Who does this fellow think he is that I will leap at his every command?" and he remained seated at the producer's command as the rest of the huge assembly leapt to their feet. The Greek American who was sitting at the end of his row of seats looked to his right, all the way across the Kennedy Center, at about 40 empty audience seats that had been just seconds before filled by Americans from every imaginable nationality. Near the other end of that long row, he saw one other individual ignoring the producer's command and remaining seated in his chair. It turned out it was a Greek American whom he knew. It was further anecdotal evidence that Hellenes tend to balk at complying with arbitrary commands.

Another striking contrast along these lines has been observed between Hellenes and non-Hellenes. When invited to a White House event at which the president or vice president would speak, non-Hellenes tended to welcome the invitation and were typically quite impressed by whatever the president or vice president had to say. In contrast, Hellenes welcome enthusiastically the invitation to the White House but when asked what they thought of the presentation by the president or vice president, they are not shy about telegraphing that they believe that they could have done a better job than the commander in chief.

Strong Women

An example of the strength of Greek women involves a funny story about an old immigrant who fit a stereotypical mold of the first half of the 20th century—an old, short, sweet, self-effacing grandmother, wearing all black, speaking English with a very thick accent. Such women seemed to be constantly cooking or baking for family, guests, or anyone who came into their home.

After shopping for groceries one day, a small town policeman who knew this woman saw her driving her car home. He saw her car hit a man, knock him down, and continue on. A little later, the policeman went to her front door and told the grandmother (*yiayia*) what had happened. Very sweetly she smiled and, in her very thick Greek accent, answered with words that became famous in that Greek community for decades. She sweetly said, "Beep, beep, three times, no move, I fix, God damn."

As one Greek American male said, "I have met shy Greek women, but never a weak one."

Strong women have a history in Hellenism. Homer told the possibly mythical story of warrior women called the Amazons. Also, during the Greek War of Independence from the Ottoman occupation in the early 19th century, a woman, known as Bouboulina, was a famous naval commander and war heroine. As well, as mentioned earlier, the Greek women on Crete who fought the Nazis, as their husbands and sons fought on the mainland, were so effective that the Nazis singled many of them out for execution.

Speaking of Crete, the Greek Minoan civilization on the island in 2700 BC worshipped a Mother Goddess. And some Greek Americans humorously believe that this history affected the subconscious of Cretan women. In the mid-1900s, a Greek American man whose family was from Crete listened to his wife take charge and tell the family what they were going to do. She left the room and he turned to his children and with a smile said, "In ancient Crete, their God was a woman." He then humorously added, "And today's Cretan women have never forgotten it."

One of the best testaments to the strength of Greek women came in early April 2020, during the beginning of the worldwide COVID-19 pandemic. Greek Prime Minister Kyriakos Mitsotakis stood out as one of the world leaders in his immediate enforcement of strict human separation and quarantine practices, the tactic that was best stemming the spread of the virus at the time.

However, he then stood out in ways that were reminiscent of the Golden Age with actions that were unprecedented, effective, and built on an unusually outstanding characteristic of the Greek people. And it displayed a unique characteristic of Greeks. His tweet read,

> *Our brave police are needed in vital posts in our fight against the virus. From today I entrust the wise Greek women to enforce the quarantine.*

A government announcement was issued saying, "The amendment to the current quarantine law transfers the power of issuing the necessary permits primarily to mothers and grandmothers, as well as wives and sisters where there is no mother or grandmother." Particularly in the Hellenic tradition, who is not going to listen to their mothers and grandmother (*yiayia*)?!

Deputizing Greek women assured the enforcement of quarantines. Other European countries that didn't react as quickly nor utilize the inherent respect Greeks have for their grandmothers to enforce their lockdown had dramatically higher new cases per day. On a per capita basis, Greece's system compared tremendously well with other European nations and much better than the United States.

Another question on the aforementioned survey that compared Greek Americans to non-Greek Americans involved the relationship of husbands and wives. The question asked, "If a man and woman head of household disagreed about something, regardless of who would appear to win, would the woman win a majority of the time?" This question elicited a 20 percent yes response from the non-Greeks and an 80 percent yes from the Greek Americans.

This result of the woman usually winning surprises many non-Greeks who say that from the outside Greek women are perceived as being solicitous, particularly to their husbands. This might be explained by the observation of one Greek American man who said, "I think generations ago Greek husbands and their wives made a subconscious deal. We said if you let us look like we are in charge, we are happy for you to be actually in charge."

This characteristic of Hellenic wives caused a humorous situation in this account of two couples having dinner together. One couple, both of whom were Greek American, came to their *koumbari*'s home for dinner. The visiting *koumbaro* was told of the survey results regarding dominant Greek women. The host then said, "I think it is true, your mother dominated your father and you saw my mother dominate my father." The guest said, "Yes, I agree in both cases." The host then said, "And your wife dominates you?" The *koumbaro* responded, "Yes, she does." At that point the guest's wife hit the guest's arm with the back of her hand and said emphatically, "I do not." The guest then muttered, "Well, she doesn't really." The host then laughed and said to the guest's wife, "You just demonstrated the validity of the survey."

Work Ethic

Contrary to the press that unfairly criticized the Greek people during their recent Great Depression, the Greek people have one of the strongest work ethics in the world. To verify that contention one can look to the record of virtually all Greeks living in economies that are strongly based on the concept of meritocracy.

The experience of Michael Psarakis, who was born in the late 1800s in Greece and settled in Washington, DC, was not unusual. After working 12-hour days on any job that would pay, he saved enough to buy a very small restaurant on K Street downtown. Once his restaurant opened, he was there from early morning until late evening seven days a week. One of his children mentioned as an adult, it is great that Dad retired as an old man because as we were growing up, we barely saw him. For Psarakis and many of his generation, such a work schedule was necessary for his or her children to grow up in a home and go to college. For their children, no sacrifice was too much.

Even in today's world, this work ethic remains for many Hellenes. When asked by young people about how one secures a job and moves up in the office of a senator or member of the House, I give the following advice. My recommendation is quite readily followed by most young Hellenes and frequently considered out of the question by some non-Hellenes.

My advice is that because everyone wants to work on Capitol Hill it is very hard to find a job and one must therefore take any job at any level one can find. I warn against being one of the Capitol Hill employees, I recall from my youth as a Capitol Hill staffer, who injures their progress by saying things such as, "I didn't get a college degree to answer phones." I recommend that after securing that job one must show up every day at least 15 minutes before one is told to show up. Also, one must work at least 30 minutes after you were supposed to leave. Finally, one should mention to the boss that if there is any task on his or her shoulders that you might be able to handle for them, that you would be happy to do so during your after hours in the office when you have finished with your official tasks. Those who do this move up within six months to a year.

The world media suggested during Greece's Great Depression that the Greek people were somehow lazy and weren't properly working as compared to Germans, for example. A closer examination of the data reported by the European Central Bank in 2013 will reveal that, in fact, the median household net worth of the Greek people is roughly twice that of the median net worth of German households. The particularly strong work ethic of the Greek people manifests itself in different ways in different economies.

Kazantzakis captured the Greek work ethic and drive. In the prologue of *Report to Greco*, Kazantzakis, as an old man, describes the drive in his life in a conversation with his dead grandfather. He says,

> *(Kazantzakis) Grandfather, give me a command.*
> *(Grandfather) Reach what you can my son. (Kazantzakis)*
> *Grandfather, give me a more difficult, a more Cretan*
> *command. (Grandfather) Reach what you cannot.*
> *(Kazantzakis) So, this is what you want, this is where*
> *you are pushing me, where you have always pushed me. I*
> *heard your command both day and night and fought as*
> *hard as I could to reach what I could not. This I set as my*
> *duty. Whether I have succeeded or not is for you to tell me.*
> *Grandfather, I stand erect before you and I wait. The battle*
> *draws to a close and I make my report. This is where and*
> *how I fought. I fell wounded and lost heart but did not*
> *desert. Though my teeth clattered with fear I bound my*
> *forehead tightly with a red handkerchief to hide the blood*
> *and I returned to the assault. Listen, therefore, Grandfather*
> *to my report. Listen to my life and judge me. If I fell*
> *wounded but allowed no one to learn of my suffering. If I*
> *never turned my back on the enemy, please give me your*
> *blessings.*

Some of that Kazantzakis mentality could be seen in the Greek Americans of the mid-1900s. Many had it so tough that they thought giving sympathy to a child encountering difficulties could limit what that child could achieve. A good example is a story my third cousin Dr. George Hatsis tells with a laugh. After becoming the first in his family to graduate from college, he went on to dental school. He had virtually burned himself out by going to school full time, working at a rest home for people with incurable diseases, and working some nights unloading beer kegs from trains in brutally cold Milwaukee, Wisconsin. Knowing how proud his family was of him, he called his parents to apologize for being on the verge of quitting, but he just couldn't do it anymore.

His father, who had a stint as a coal miner, responded by saying with a laugh, "George, if you need some help, use your other hand"—implying that he and certainly his son could do with one hand what George was complaining about. George sucked it up, succeeded, and laughs about it now.

It should have been no surprise to George because his father, Charlie Hatsis, was known to give voice to what virtually every Hellene thought. He said, "Your grandparents came to this country and just got their toe in the door. Your mother and I were able to get the whole foot in but I expect you to own the house." Any challenge George took on in life was charged with the words of his father ringing in his ears, "Just remember George, you are as good as any and better than many."

For Hellenes, particularly of George's generation but for others as well, this proximity to very difficult times in Greece and in America is a tremendous mood-boosting blessing. When life seems too much to bear, all we have to do is ask ourselves what our grandparents or parents would have given to be in our situation.

Creators of Contests

This use of the word "contests" does not address the fact that nowhere in the world were there routinely scheduled athletic competitions until ancient Greece's establishment of the Olympics. This Olympic competition was a very serious matter. It included an "Olympic Truce" that brought all wars in the known world to a halt so that each country's best athletes could safely travel to Greece to compete. As you will see, in addition to this serious Greek competition, Greeks in Greece and Greek Americans just love to compete.

Every New Year, many Greeks make or purchase a loaf of New Year's bread that has a coin baked somewhere within. The bread is called *vasilopita*. This is a religious tradition based on St. Basil's Day, January 1 (Basil in Greek is *Vassilis* and bread in Greek is *pita*—thus *vasilopita*—Basil's bread). At a New Year's event, the Greek bread is cut with a piece for the house and for each person present, eldest to youngest. Whoever gets the coin in their piece of bread is said to have a blessed new year. Many coin winners carry that coin with them for that blessed year, just in case.

Also, in the New Year, the first person to step foot in some Greek people's houses becomes the "first footer" who brings good luck to that household and is given money by the homeowner. Additionally, in early January (Epiphany), the Greek Orthodox Church celebrates Christ's baptism in the river Jordan. Some Greek Orthodox priests, whose parishes are near a river, lake, or ocean, even in the cold north, gather the parishioners for an Epiphany competition. The priest throws a cross in the water and the teenagers of that church dive in the water and try to retrieve it.

At Easter, there is yet another competition. Greeks dye hard-boiled eggs dark red, signifying the blood of Christ, and then give them out to each family member or guest celebrating. The family or guests then begin crashing the pointed end of their egg into the pointed end of someone else's egg. The same is done with the rounded end. The person propelling his or her egg says in Greek, "*Christos Anesti,*" meaning "Christ has risen." When the person responds by propelling his or her egg into the other person's egg, he or she says,

"*Alithos Anesti,*" meaning "truly He has risen." The person whose egg survives the battering usually gets some monetary reward. The competition is always fun and the center of attention.

In the mid-20th century, in the Greek Orthodox subculture in America, another unintentional competition took place at Easter. It occurred just before midnight when all the church lights were turned off and the parishioners held a candle, yet to be lit. Near midnight the priest would emerge from the altar with the holy flame, signifying Christ's resurrection, with his candle to begin singing in Greek the wonderful hymn, *Christ Has Risen from the Dead.*

A few minutes before the priest emerged, a muted rumbling sound could be heard throughout the pitch-black church. It was caused by a good number of very old, Greek-born *yiayias* moving from their seats in the pews to the aisles and up the aisles in order to get as close as possible to the altar's opening where the priest would soon emerge with his lit candle. These *yiayias* believed that the person who got the light first from the priest's holy flame would have a blessed life throughout the following 12 months. Typically, the priest would emerge holding his lit candle forward as he leaned back protecting

himself from the many candles of these eager *yiayias* being thrust toward him. Once a *yiayia* secured the flame and her coming year of blessedness, they would all return to their pews as the flame was passed to each candle in the church. In the aftermath, with all those lit candles in the hands of adults and children in close pews, it would not be uncommon to catch the faint smell of singed hair.

Today, this spreading of the holy flame is distributed in a very organized and "American" way. The priest lights the candle of a church board member or the altar boys and they pass it on. It is much more "civilized" but not nearly as much fun.

In the early 1900s, a Greek American godparent would select his or her godchild's name at the baptism. The child's mother was not allowed to attend the baptism, initiating yet another competition. The children of the family's friends in attendance at the baptism would then race to the home of the child's mother to be the first to tell her the child's name and to be given a monetary reward. These days, of course, the child's parents do the naming, and both attend the baptism.

Even at Thanksgiving, a totally American holiday, some Greek Americans cannot control their competitive zest. For decades, they've had a competition with a Greek sounding name called *Yantis* that begins with breaking the turkey's wishbone. It is a bit complicated but can go on for days and can be very nerve-racking until someone wins.

In Greece different regions have slightly varied activities at holiday events. On someone's name day (the celebration of the saint after whom the person is named), it is tradition to wish that person in Greek *chronia polla* (many years). And on the island of Crete many people in addition pull that person's ear lobe.

I know of no study comparing nationalities and their contests. However, when one considers the coin in the bread, the first foot in the door, the cross in the water, the unbroken red egg, *yiayias* elbowing for the first light from a candle, racing to tell a mother her baby's name, and *Yantis*—from our observation in America, none seems to come close to the number of competitions enjoyed by Hellenes.

Family Togetherness

A Greek American who married a girl whose family origin was German and British noticed some striking differences between how the families conducted themselves. In the wife's family, if relatives gathered in a room to visit, there were numerous quiet conversations between two people going on around the room. In contrast, if the same number of Greek relatives were gathered in a similar room, there tended to be one big conversation into which everyone would loudly jump. It was no surprise when a Greek American US Ambassador to Belgium, Tom Korologos, asked his 16 guests sitting around his embassy's formal dining room table in Brussels if they would mind having one conversation. He said he found it more interesting, not realizing that his Hellenic subculture had led him to that unusual practice.

This gregarious characteristic is also seen in Greece where the following was said. If in Norway a person is solitarily walking along the water's edge, it is said, "What a deep person he is." But if the same is seen in Greece it is observed, "What is wrong with that fellow?"

The Greek American who married the girl whose family was from Germany and Britain also noticed that when one entered his wife's household, each family member was in a different place. One might be reading a book in his or her room, another working in the garden, another reading the paper in the den, and another in the kitchen. The Greek American pointed out that in most Greek American households, the family would be gathered together, usually in the kitchen visiting, discussing loudly, and laughing with each other.

Greeks emphasizing points with hand gestures, facial expressions, or fluctuating enthusiastic voice inflection are sometimes misinterpreted by non-Hellenes as anger. Some even describe it as yelling although the voice gets no louder. Enjoying some peaceful quiet time? Not very often!

One such misinterpretation of some of these Greek actions showed itself to me through the former Congressman John Porter when I was with him in Athens. The Greek Government sent a car to the hotel to take him to a meeting with a cabinet minister. When he returned he told me, "You might want to tell your friend, the minister, that the driver he sent apparently has some serious personal problems." With concern I said, "Of course, what did he do?" He said, "More than once he rolled down the car window, gestured with his hands out the window, and yelled at other drivers." I then explained, "That's actually not unusual in Greece."

Interestingly, although such yelling, particularly in traffic, is more common in Greece, taking the next step and throwing a punch is never seen. Unlike in America, the use of physical violence against each other in Greece is virtually unheard of.

There are many situations when a non-Greek marries a Greek and gets welcomed and completely absorbed into Hellenic culture. Some embrace it fully. In one family, this was so true that when their eldest child was nine years old, he ran up to his Greek American father one day and said with astonishment, "Dad, did you know Mom is not Greek?"

CHAPTER 6

Conclusion

In place of the conclusions to which the above information should lead you, I will instead just list the many accomplishments of the extraordinary Greek people. Before you read it, don't forget that the philosopher Isocrates said, "Being Greek is not so much a term of birth as of mentality." A scan of the list should make the point that the people who made all these things happen throughout history are truly extraordinary.

A review of major strides forward finds that the Greeks:

1. In Crete created indoor plumbing 3,000 years before the British spoke English;
2. Of the Golden Age invented a myriad of breakthrough advances for civilization, 2,000 years before the wheel came to some continents;
3. Created the governmental system used by the greatest nation the world has known, the United States;
4. Refused to surrender to WWII's Axis Forces when standing nearly alone in opposition;
5. Were the first to inflict a defeat against WWII's Axis Forces in Europe;
6. Killed more Nazis in one day (Battle of Crete) than any day to that point in the year-and-a-half-old war;
7. Were the only Nazi-occupied country to publicly oppose the Holocaust as it was happening;
8. Were the only non-world-power credited with stopping Hitler's planned world of horror;

9. Are the only nationality with a word to describe their highly practiced virtue, *philotimo*;
10. Lead the world in fatherly responsibility;
11. Lead Europe in holding their culture in the highest esteem; and
12. Were identified by President Kennedy as knowing the true meaning of happiness, when he said, happiness to the Greeks is "the full use of your powers along lines of excellence." (quoted in a 1963 press conference)

Greek Americans:
1. Led in Rhodes Scholar percentage in the US Congress in the 1970s;
2. Were the first group in modern times able to secure the US Capitol Rotunda for a living person;
3. Are the only nationality to have two generations of the same family receive Princeton University's prestigious Pyne Honor Award;
4. Established the presidential primary fundraising record for all elections before 1988;
5. Led a recent American effort to revive citizen support for democracy;
6. Rose in one generation from the bottom to be among the top nationalities in America in education and income;
7. Were the only nationality able to move Congress to overrule the White House on a major foreign policy issue in modern history; and
8. Are the only nationality (other than the Irish) to arrange to meet with every US president every year for over 33 years.

In addition, positive aspects of the Hellenic culture include:
1. Having strong and spontaneous familial relationships with most other Greeks;
2. Possessing a strong understanding of the path to a good life;
3. Tending to be quite self-confident;
4. Being born into a culture that underscores the importance of dignity;

5. Finding a lifestyle that leads in health and longevity;
6. Not being inclined to blindly follow untested leadership;
7. Having a spiritual head considered to be most "Christ-like" by a world leader;
8. Feeling pride whenever seeing the name of a person of his or her nationality doing well;
9. Enjoying an inclination to seek excellence;
10. Being inclined to play the hand dealt rather than see themselves as victims;
11. Unquestionably sacrificing greatly for a family member or *koumbari*;
12. Enjoying a safety net of immediate family, extended family, *koumbari*, and friends;
13. Enjoying a very low rate of alcoholism and dementia;
14. Being part of a group of successful, law-abiding people who more readily trust each other; and
15. Having strong feelings of obligation to those who sacrificed for them and having courage.

These things did not happen by coincidence or chance. It is much like the fact that Jewish people make up less than one percent of the American people yet constitute nearly 20 percent of *Fortune* magazine's list of the 200 wealthiest people in America. Something is causing it to happen.

There is no question that Hellenism has provided Hellenes with extraordinarily good lives. Most Hellenes realize this and appreciate their circumstances greatly. DNA tests of recent years suggest that much of the genius of Hellenism is the result of the passage, from generation to generation, of information and material that may not be contained in DNA. Those of us who have benefited from the value of Hellenism have an obligation to maintain this heritage for our progeny and for others interested in Hellenism. We have an obligation to give them the same benefits with which we have been blessed.

My *koumbara* Vanessa Andris stated best my thoughts in summary. She said,

> *This is a loss that neither Hellenes nor the world can afford. Survival does depend on adaptation, changing. And it also requires bringing the best of the species, of a people, forward. Each culture has admirable attributes to pass on through generations. Knowing that, what Hellenes have is well worth all its sons and daughters carrying forth. It's my dearest wish that they and others reading this will realize these attributes—to preserve the best of this world and reap life's greatest rewards forever.*

The consequences of the loss of Hellenism for Hellenes and non-Hellenes alike can be better appreciated with the words of the longest-serving US Supreme Court Justice, William O. Douglas, whom I knew while I was a student. Paraphrasing his words for Hellenism, "As nightfall does not come all at once, neither does the loss of Hellenism. In both instances there is a twilight where everything remains seemingly unchanged and it is in such twilight that we must be aware of change in the air, however slight, lest we become unwitting victims of the darkness."

SECTION II

Hellenism's Value
to Some of the Most
Successful Hellenes

His Eminence Archbishop Elpidophoros of the Greek Orthodox Church of America

As the Greek Orthodox Archbishop of America, it is my pleasure to introduce what follows: reflections and appreciations of Hellenes about their culture, language, and legacy.

Each offering is different and presents unique perspectives on what Hellenism means, both to themselves and to the world at large. The diversity of the contributors' backgrounds makes the meaning of their remarks all the richer.

As a Greek of Constantinople, where Hellenism received its perfection in the Faith of Christ, I see a broad spectrum of Hellenic values throughout history. As an example, the German language received its first standardization from the translation of the New Testament from Greek by Martin Luther. And then, centuries later, the German language influenced the creation of *Katharevousa*—the formal academic language of Greece in the 19th and 20th centuries. This ebb and flow of Greek influence is ubiquitous in the history of the world.

The linguistic magnificence of the Greeks—from Homer to Kazantzakis—has had an amazing influence on the world. But language is the expression of the mind. And the *phronema* and *nous* of Greece have shaped Western civilization in the most significant ways through the centuries. Virtually every philosophical and scientific category employs the intellectual legacies of Greece. Whether through something as complex as dialectical analysis, or through something as simple as the syllogism, the Greek mind has made its impact on the modern world in ways many have forgotten.

The texts that follow remind us of what the Hellenes have dedicated to our values over the ages, and how they are just as relevant today as they were millennia ago. Let us listen to these voices and remember, so that we may pass along this wisdom to the future.

Art Agnos, Former Mayor of San Francisco

As the first of my family to be born in America, my story is one of dual heritage ... the first proudly American ... and the second proudly Greek. And it was my immigrant Greek parents who manifested the power of that Greek heritage for me with their commitment to my success the only way they knew how—with unconditional love and support no matter what the challenge. In doing so, they blended the "old country" customs and mores with their new exposure to American values and culture.

The common denominator in that blend was the notion of *philotimo*, meaning a "love of honor." While there are many interpretations of this classic Greek trait, for me it simply means to live an honorable life by treating one's fellow human beings with respect, equality, and courtesy thereby earning the right for similar treatment in return. That sense of *philotimo* was intertwined with the ever-present understanding that as a Greek, we were the descendants of a glorious ancient civilization, whose philosophy, art, and governance culture are on display all over the world, and therefore destined for continued greatness.

No matter where I am at any given time, a Greek name in the media immediately grabs my attention to make a quick assessment of the actions of that fellow Greek. Did they do good or bad? Do their actions bring pride to the community—or God forbid, shame?

That lesson came at home from my mother and father who began to relay the culture and values of the old country to me before I could talk.

On very rare occasions, I would go to see a movie with my father. At the end of the movie, he would insist that we remain seated until all the credits were completed. And then if he spotted a Greek name in the credits, he would lean over to me and whisper, "See that Greek name? That's why it was such a good movie! Now we can go."

Sometimes we had to wait until the credits scrolled down to the name of the film's caterer before the inevitable paternal pronouncement made it possible for us to leave a nearly empty movie house.

A Greek name in any public setting triggered the same lectures again and again until they became indelible. Indeed, those repetitive lessons have played a significant role in my response to the question, "How did the son of a peasant Greek immigrant leave Massachusetts for California on a Greyhound bus with $500 in his pocket, ride nonstop for three days and two nights to arrive in San Francisco not knowing anybody west of the Mississippi River, get elected to the California legislature 10 years later, and then mayor 10 years after that?"

The answer may be complex, but the one indisputable and dominant ingredient is the confidence and pride of identity as Hellenes transmitted to us daily first by our parents and then regularly reinforced by our church, art, music, and world history.

Five years of Greek school, supplemented with Sunday school, enhanced with parental stories gave me an early sense of identity and pride that has sustained and energized me throughout my career and life especially when encountering prejudice and discrimination from hostile, know-nothing American groups. When someone called me stupid or called me names as a youngster, my mother would cheer me up with stories of how Greeks were among the highest educated people today, and our people probably taught my bullies' ancestors how to read and write.

Just six years before my father arrived as a 15-year-old laborer recruited to work on the construction of the railroads in 1915, the city of San Francisco's newspaper—where his son would become the city's 39th mayor in 1988—had a front-page story warning American women not to marry a Greek because he may leave her to return to his real Greek family as soon as he made enough money (*SF Call Bulletin*, 1909).

My first experience outside of the cocoon of my Greek culture involved going to school as a five-year-old being raised by parents who, along with my newly arrived relatives lived together in one house and only spoke Greek at home. Upon arrival at elementary school, it was quickly determined that I did not speak English. I was promptly sent home with a note summoning my parents. My father who spoke limited English—my mother spoke none—immediately responded with a powerful explanation to the school authorities: "First we taught him the language we know best and now we send him to you for you to teach him the language you know best."

That simple truth emanated from my parents who wanted their first-born son to identify with his heritage and be proud of it. This commitment held even with relatively insignificant things like school lunch. My classmates usually ate peanut butter and jelly sandwiches alternating with baloney on white bread. My lunch box would have a sandwich made of aromatic slices of lamb on dark bread and feta cheese or a portion of pastitsio, Kalamata olives and sometimes a small thermos of lentil soup.

My classmates would screech at the sight and smell of my home-made Greek lunch whereupon I would go home later that day to beg my mother for a baloney or peanut butter and jelly sandwich for a school lunch. She was shocked and dismayed because she could not understand why her son wanted tasteless items like that instead of her prized lamb and lentil soup until I told her why. Her response was immediate and strong, "… tomorrow give them a taste of your Greek lunch and see if they want baloney anymore." That did it—my lunch became the favorite target for a lunch trade in my elementary school class.

At the age of 10, I started to work in my father's small hat cleaning and shoeshine shop. As we stood side by side shining various business executive's shoes, I remember him leaning over and whispering in Greek that I was to be the first of my family to go to college so I could be the one having *my* shoes shined instead of shining someone else's shoes for the rest of my life.

My father would reinforce that message at every opportunity. On Sundays after church services, he would take me to the parish hall to listen to a lecture from some important community leader. A humble man, he would position himself at the back of the room with me on his shoulders so I could see over the seated spectators with a clear line of sight to the important speaker. His sweet desire was a hope that, with a direct view, some of the speaker's best qualities might rub off on to his son in the back of the room.

Maybe it did, but my father never got to see that because he died of cancer when I was 16 in 1955. At the time we had no health care and Medicare did not exist. And there was no money for visiting home nurses or any other kind of support for our family.

So, my mother would stay home to nurse him while I went to

open and operate the shoeshine store from 6:00 a.m. until 10:00 a.m. Just before she left the house to come downtown to take over at the store so I could go to school late, she would call me at the store and then leave the home phone off the hook by his pillow with his medication. And at the store, I would leave that phone off the hook as well. Once at the store, she would use the off the hook land line telephone to communicate with him and monitor his condition while I went to school for a compressed day of classes.

After the death of my father, my mother took over the full operation of the store while I gave my full attention to my studies in anticipation of college applications. It also gave me more time for my social development and dating. That was when I first encountered a different kind of overt prejudice. I could not date certain girls because their fathers said that I was "too Mediterranean"—whatever that meant—not to mention my strange religion represented by priests wearing long beards and big, black stovepipe hats.

Even though I never felt like I belonged socially in college, it was a dream to escape the trauma of my father's long fight with cancer and my high school schedule. Living away from home in dormitory and school where everybody was "American," I learned how to handle myself eating in a restaurant for the first time. At home, my mother's kitchen was the only restaurant I knew. So, when my new roommates invited me to go out to an Italian restaurant for pasta and pizza, I panicked and called home for instruction. "Eat slow and watch how your companions do it and then copy them." I ordered a pizza and robustly sprinkled spices like garlic and oregano on it, but that strange little bottle full of crushed red pepper flakes I had never seen before hit my throat and stomach like a flamethrower. Lotta laughs over that in the dorm.

After college, I left to pursue my future in a city on the other side of the country. My widowed mother, who was never totally familiar with the ways of America, gave me the only advice she thought could help me. She said, "Your father is gone and I do not know the ways of this country well enough to advise you in your career. All I can tell you is to find wise, educated Greek men and women in our community out there and use their advice."

And I did, going as often as I could to what I referred to as "Greeky" events to seek advice in the midst of the affectionate warmth of my community.

These experiences continued to form the essence of my identity as a Greek American and as an elected official. Indeed, Greek history and personal experience as a Greek American, rather than any intellectual ideology, framed my personal and political philosophy.

When immigrant children today enter school not speaking English, I am reminded of my own experience entering school unable to speak or understand English.

When I learn of discrimination in our society today, I remember that in the early years of San Francisco, the newspapers of the city I was mayor of once warned the women of San Francisco not to marry a Greek.

When I read of sick people who can't afford health care, I think of my father alone in bed with the phone constantly off the hook to allow my mother to speak with him as his only link to health care.

During difficult stretches of my life, I leaned in on my intellectual and cultural ally in the form of my heritage in general and *philotimo* in particular to sustain me.

Never did that value become more vivid than in my first campaign for mayor in 1987 when I was an underdog candidate challenging the scion of an old and powerful political family. Early in the race, I was attacked by my opponent, causing a huge drop in the polls. Political experts recommended that I drop out to avoid the ignominy of defeat. Upon learning of this, my mother, who still was not comfortable with English, spoke to me alone in Greek to remind me with great passion who we were as a family and who I was as her son—a Greek man imbued with the heroic tradition of men of Sparta and the women of Zalongo who never surrendered when faced with the prospect of defeat.

Her message was simple—never, never, never give up.

I took my mother's words to heart and refused to quit. Six months later we won the election in a huge landslide with 73 percent of the vote. My mother held the Bible as I took the oath of office on inauguration day 1988.

At a formal city dinner honoring then Soviet Union President Mikhail Gorbachev, I was seated next to him and decided to ask about Moscow's Mayor Gavril Popov who was of Greek descent and occasionally critical of him in the media. Through an interpreter, he described him as impatient and critical of the changes he was making in Russian society at that time.

I leaned over and said, "Well, Mr. President, when you return to Moscow, tell him you have a new Greek friend in the mayor of San Francisco. And if he doesn't start showing more *philotimo*, you will send for me to educate him about the meaning of *philotimo* in his mother's Greek language."

The interpreter could not explain what *philotimo* meant, so I did. And when I finished, Gorbachev loudly clapped his hands with delight and in pretty good English said, "I'm gonna tell him as soon as I get back!"

One year later, Mayor Gavril Popov visited the US at the invitation of the White House. I used the occasion to invite the mayor to visit me as a fellow Greek in San Francisco. He accepted and when he arrived, I met him at the airport with a full-blown diplomatic red-carpet ceremony that equaled the welcoming reception for Gorbachev. Why? Because he was Greek, of course!

The mayor's office also became a place of ethnic engagement with the occasional arrival of Greek tourists expecting to see the new Greek mayor. At first, security personnel would attempt to usher them out of the reception area of the office. No chance. They were not leaving until they could see the Greek mayor in person.

When I became aware of this, the policy was changed immediately with instructions to escort every Greek visitor to my office for a tour and greeting from me if I was anywhere in the vicinity. Scouring all those movie credits with my father a long, long time ago made it easy to understand what my role was in those visits from my *patrioti* who came from all over the world.

In more recent times, the image of ordinary Greek Americans attending a mayoral campaign fundraiser in distant cities like Boston, New York, Chicago, Phoenix, Seattle, Sacramento, Los Angeles, and San Diego to elect a Greek mayor in San Francisco most of them would never see after he was elected was indelibly etched in my mind. And I knew why. Even if San Francisco was far from where they lived, they were proud to support one of their own to be the mayor of such an important city in the world.

Cognizant of those early lessons of my father and mother, the dominant thought in my mind throughout my career and life was to make sure that everyone—but especially Greeks—would be aware and proud of one of their own serving his city and country with *philotimo*.

And today it continues.

My son, who learns from me today as I once did from my father and mother, is teaching his son and daughter.

Maria Allwin, The Archbishop Iakovos Leadership 100 Fund, Inc. Secretary; Philanthropist

I wake up every morning, a Greek American mother, daughter, *yiayia*, and friend. Whenever I face a challenge, I'm reminded of my family making the journey to America on a boat with no money, family, Google, or cell phone! They succeeded because they brought their strong Greek Orthodox faith and culture, and this gives me strength to carry on with my day. I also get great happiness from being with other Greeks, as I know the company will lead to light-hearted fun. Keeping my faith in my heart, I face each day with a smile on my face and try to be a beacon of strength for my family. We Greeks have a dynamic culture that permeates my everyday life, including the signature of my emails, "*filikia*."

John Angelos, Chairman and CEO and MLB Control Person, Baltimore Orioles; President and COO, Mid-Atlantic Network

Like so many other Americans whose ancestors came to this country in search of a better life, I am the product of hardworking and entrepreneurial Greek immigrants. I can trace my Hellenic heritage through the parents of both my mother and my father, who came to this country with only their dreams, ambition, and desire to build a better life for themselves and their families. And this country gave them an opportunity.

Like many other immigrant stories, my Angelos and Kousouris forebears worked hard to establish themselves in America. They began first as small business people, then worked in factories and steel mills, then became owners of several restaurants and taverns, and even operated the hot dog truck outside Memorial Stadium during Orioles and Colts games. Successive generations have stood upon that foundation of hard work, as family members attained higher education as attorneys and as other professionals.

The ancient Greeks prioritized several core values as ingredients for a successful life. Those values include intelligence, excellence, hospitality, and loyalty, and they are values that I strive to embody in my life and work.

The US is fortunate to have the largest ethnically Greek population outside of Greece, as our community numbers more than three million. We have made enormous contributions to civic life—to the arts, sports, business, politics, and every other aspect of contemporary American life. These contributions would not have been possible if not for the tradition of hard work being grounded in the values of our Greek heritage, and I believe that hard work will continue to inform and guide the vision for each generation to come.

Peter Baker, Chief White House Correspondent, the *New York Times*; Author

My father's father arrived in the United States from Piraeus, Greece, on a ship called the SS *Patris* on October 10, 1909. He was 17 years old, a slight boy of 5 foot 6, not quite yet a man, with no discernible skills or education or gifts other than a determination to flee Ottoman repression and make a better life for himself in the land of the free.

On the manifest, they listed his name as Panayotis Bakertzoglou, which soon became Peter Baker, and it was him for whom I was named. He worked laying railroad tracks, later became a candymaker, and eventually owned a small restaurant. He settled in West Virginia, where he met and married a young Greek girl named Argiro Photinou. He was known as a kind man who believed in treating others as he would want to be treated.

My *pappou* never had an extra nickel in his life and never believed in borrowing money but was always ready to help those in need. Lights in their house were kept off at night, they rarely took trips out of town, there were few if any real indulgences. But he managed to send his son, my father, Eleftherios Peter Baker, to Harvard Law School. In just one generation, from a penniless immigrant to an Ivy League-trained lawyer, a classic American story, and one that shaped my upbringing.

Growing up in a Greek American family like that, you learned to take nothing for granted and to appreciate the opportunities of a new land. You learned that nothing is given to you and everything is earned, that talent is wonderful but hard work is the most vital ingredient for success, that honesty and integrity and decency and generosity and compassion and perseverance and family are more important than anything else. When he was facing a challenge, my dad always asked himself what his father would do. When I face a challenge, I always ask myself what my dad would do. That is a lucky inheritance indeed.

Drake G. Behrakis, President of Marwick Associates; Chairman of the Board, National Hellenic Society

Hellenism has impacted me from birth. As a young second generation Greek American born into a close-knit Greek community, I watched and observed those around me as they lived their daily lives. As a professional, I began to chart my course, guided by those values and beliefs instilled in me, putting practice into play. Finally, as a father, husband, and community leader, my challenge is whatever I do, it's now based on continuing to build upon the legacy of my forefathers to ensure it passes on to the next generation.

Lily Haseotes Bentas, CEO and Chairperson, Cumberland Farms; Philanthropist

I grew up in the small rural town of Cumberland, Rhode Island, where we were the only Greek family.

Both my parents were immigrants from Greece. My father, Vasilios S. Haseotes, came to Ellis Island at the turn of the 20th century as a young teenager from the Epirus section of northern Greece. My mother, Aphrodite Bassis Haseotes, came with her mother and sister in the early 1900s to join their father who had immigrated earlier from the village of Nymphaion in Thessaly.

They came like most Greek immigrants at that time to build a better life for themselves and their families to live the American Dream. They brought with them their culture and values, and the history of Greece, along with their Greek Orthodox religion.

Not only was religion important to my parents but our involvement in the Greek church also became part of the social fabric of our lives. We bonded with other immigrant families that shared the same culture, background, and values, and many of those bonds have lasted a lifetime and still exist today.

Growing up as the only Greek family in Cumberland, we faced many challenges. For example, our classmates found it strange when my mother would keep us out of school on Greek Good Friday and other Greek holidays.

We all had daily chores on the farm. This gave us a strong work ethic along with a sense of responsibility, knowing that how we acted had an impact on other aspects of our family life. My parents also wanted their children educated and they instilled that in us, along with a strong work ethic, a drive to succeed, and to be honest and good citizens.

Not only did I work on the farm, but during high school I worked in the first dairy store that my family opened in 1957. Over the years, I held various management positions in the company and became chairman and CEO in 1990. At that time, we were employing over 8,000 people and operating convenience/gasoline stores throughout the Northeast and Florida and our Gulf Oil division was operating in over 20 states in the northern and mid-sections of the United States.

Businesses face many challenges; industries have ups and downs. Family businesses have an additional set of challenges unique to them. As I look back over the years, those values that were instilled in me in my younger life by my parents gave me the courage and will to face these different challenges.

We grew up proud of our country and our heritage and I was extremely proud when the Oxi Foundation honored my father for his service as an American soldier in World War I, where he fought in France and was decorated by both the American and the French governments. I was equally proud when, in a subsequent year, my husband was honored for his service in World War II where he was a member of the OSS, serving part of his time in Italy.

We as Americans owe a great debt of gratitude to all the men and women of our armed forces who have given so much to defend our democracy and to protect our country, and we should never forget or take for granted the sacrifices they have made.

Congressman Gus M. Bilirakis, Member of Congress

If I had a dollar every time I've said, "I'm blessed to be of both heritages," I'd be a millionaire! The good fortune of being born in the United States where diversity is celebrated allowed me to grow up in a world in which I soaked up the customs and traditions of my Greek heritage and Orthodox faith by working with my *yiayia* and *pappou* in their bakery where I served Greek customers. I spoke to these ragged, yet proud men and women in Greek and learned about their lives and how they traded one set of hardships in a war-torn Greece for another set of hardships in the strange New World. Their resiliency and perseverance and strength of character seemed like superpowers to me! With little or no money or education, and an inability to speak the language, they were able to form a new existence for themselves and their children. They worked hard and became entrepreneurs, professionals, academics, artists, and political leaders. Their histories have helped inform my world view. I have endeavored to perpetuate the values of Hellenism and Orthodoxy like *philotimo* and civic responsibility for my children, friends, and congressional colleagues because they are values worth replicating. God willing, I will continue my work in the US Congress and put forth policies that celebrate all that is good and true about our heritage and faith.

The Honorable B. Theodore Bozonelis, Judge; National Vice Commander and Executive Committee Member of the Order of Saint Andrew

A Lasting Legacy of Integrity

At the turn of the century, Peter Saros left his wife, Lygeri, and young son, James, in Lira, Greece, and travelled to South Africa and Australia before settling in the United States in order to create a better future for his family. He was determined to earn, save, and create a business—to live the American Dream. It took him 10 years of hard work and separation before he called for his wife and son to join him. By that time, he not only owned properties and restaurants in Elizabeth, New Jersey, but was also a founder of St. Nicholas Greek Orthodox Church in Newark.

Together, Peter and Lygeri had seven more children, two girls and five boys. Four sons served and saw action in World War II before returning home safely. The whole family and their children's children, all of Greek heritage, lived together in a very large home on a street called DeHart Place in Elizabeth. It was a mansion to me as a five-year-old, as I was one of the children's children, and Peter and Lygeri Saros were my *pappou* and *yiayia*.

Their story and sacrifices for a better life are the stories of many Greek families who immigrated to the United States. It was an inspiration to all who followed the same brave path, including my father, Theodore Bozonelis, who was also born in Greece, and married my mother, Ellen Saros Bozonelis. They began raising their children—my sister Phoebe and me—with all our aunts and uncles, living in that big house on DeHart Place. There, my parents, *pappou*, and *yiayia*, offered us love, affection, and security always centered in the unwavering faith of our Greek Orthodox religion.

As the years passed and DeHart Place became a memory, my *yiayia* lived with us in our new home, as my parents came to own a successful restaurant. *Yiayia* was constant in her love and caring and instilled a sense of what it meant to live a life in Christ with morals and integrity, teaching us by example through our Greek heritage. That inner strength of integrity and what it meant to be a Greek Orthodox Christian carried through to my parents, my sister, and me.

Although my parents were not college educated, they had that core of *yiayia's* common sense and work ethic which they passed on to us. They instilled in us to be fair, to never consider yourself better than others no matter background and circumstances, and to pursue a better life through our Orthodox faith. Material wealth, if obtained, was welcomed, but not required.

For my parents, that better life also meant for my sister and me to pursue an education and a professional career, which had never been available to them. We followed through, grateful for these opportunities and their support, never forgetting the lessons of our Greek heritage or our family's core values.

I met my beautiful wife, Helen Koutras, while I was in law school in Washington DC, at the Eastern Orthodox Club, an interfaith religious organization. Helen received her degree in international relations and was brought up with that same strong faith and pride in our Greek heritage. She has taught me many more lessons of what it means to be a faithful Orthodox Christian. We are one, together in Christ, with our children, Justin and Lia, and precious grandchildren.

The path I followed and all those lessons learned allowed me to achieve a career goal of serving in the judiciary. It has given me the opportunity to serve the Greek Orthodox Archdiocese and Ecumenical Patriarchate as an Archon of the Order of Saint Andrew the Apostle. It has offered me personal relationships with individuals including the late Nicholas J. Bouras who, with his wife Anna, gained considerable wealth, lived a distinguished, Christ-centered, modest and moral life, and led us all by the example of being the great benefactor to our Mother Church. I am privileged to serve as a trustee of the Nicholas J. and Anna K. Bouras Foundation which continues their legacy of philanthropy.

Remembering my *pappou* and *yiayia* and their lineage, and those lessons learned, all of us look to embrace our Greek Orthodox heritage and strive to have the highest ethics, to be fair, and to treat all others with respect. To me, that is Peter and Lygeri's lasting legacy of integrity. That is our Greek heritage.

Sylvia Mathews Burwell, President of American University

My Greek heritage is something I feel and live every day—from the food my family eats to my faith and many other aspects of my life. But for the purposes of this assignment, I will focus on two other areas of our culture that impact me every day.

First, education, which is an important concept in the Greek community and one I was reminded of all throughout my childhood. My parents consistently taught my sister and me about the importance of education, which can provide a path to a fascinating and wide world. That lesson comes to life for me every day in my role as president of American University in Washington, DC. I have a front row seat to see how an education can create opportunities for our students, faculty, and staff to create knowledge for the greater good. For this, I am grateful for how my family and our Greek background laid the foundation for my appreciation for education.

The second aspect of my Greek heritage that is integral to my life is family—a concept that is broadly defined in the Greek community. One of my favorite memories is when I first introduced my husband, Stephen, to my "family" at a 70th birthday party for my mother. I introduced him to my "aunts" and "uncles," and he kept asking how we were related. I would reply, "Well, we're not exactly blood relatives ..." We later had our wedding in his hometown of Seattle, Washington, and there were more members of my "family" there—all the way from West Virginia. To this end, my family thinks that Stephen's family is Greek: his mother is Joanne, his brother is Jim, and his niece is Georgia—so we are confident that his family is Greek, and they just don't know it. The concept of family—whether it is formed by blood or choice—is something that brings such joy to my life.

When my grandparents came to America and eventually made their way to West Virginia, they became a part of the American Dream: the opportunity to earn an honest living while providing for your family. Coming to America changed the trajectory of their lives, and in turn, the trajectory of mine. But we were encouraged to never forget where we originally came from. Being Greek is an enormous part of who we are and who we aspire to be. I am grateful for the gifts this country has given my family and for the lessons that my Greek heritage provides me every single day.

John P. Calamos Sr., Founder, Chairman, and Global Chief Investment Officer, Calamos Investments; Philanthropist

There is a quote I come back to often: "You don't know who you are unless you know where you came from." My family's Hellenic values provided the foundation for me to become the person I am today. My father was a Greek immigrant, and he and my mother didn't have the benefit of an advanced formal education; neither of them finished high school. What was more important was that they were absolutely committed to creating a better life for their family, which ultimately allowed me to pursue the American Dream. They also recognized and instilled in me the importance of community and of service.

We owned a small grocery store in Chicago, where I worked alongside my parents. Back then, neighborhood grocery stores like ours were part of the lifeblood of our Greek American community. We knew everyone who came through the door.

Faith and Hellenism were very important aspects of our family values. I didn't realize it at the time but going to church and Sunday school became a central component of my character. My experiences there instilled values that guide me to this day, values which I have come to appreciate more and more as the years pass.

I have always been a risk taker, and I know that stems from the risks my parents took to provide us with opportunities for a better life. I just went my own way and made my own mistakes. I think about that a lot. If I had always followed other peoples' advice, would I still have made the decisions that ultimately served me very well? If you want to be successful in business, if you want to innovate, if you want to follow your own path in life—you have to take risks.

I was the first in my family to go to college. I attended Illinois Tech and on a whim decided to enter its Air Force ROTC program.

I served as a combat pilot during the Vietnam War, where I flew hundreds of missions as a forward air controller. We were there to support the ground troops by controlling fighters to help them in time of need. During my Vietnam tour, I was awarded the Distinguished Flying Cross for a particularly harrowing mission. Overall, I spent five years on active duty and 12 years in the reserves flying B52s and jet fighters. I left the service as a major with lessons learned in leadership, camaraderie, and risk management … attributes that proved very valuable as I built and grew my business.

I studied the markets in my "downtime" during my military career and discovered I had a deep interest in the investment world. This eventually led me to founding Calamos Investments in the 1970s.

At the time, I was especially interested in convertible securities, and I'm truly honored to be called a pioneer in the use of convertible securities. I authored two books discussing the asset class and various investment techniques. I launched one of the first convertible funds in 1985 as a way to manage risk for clients in volatile times and also established one of the first liquid alternative funds in 1990. Today, Calamos Investments is a global asset manager, serving individuals and institutions around the world, with a continued focus on innovation. We specialize in providing risk-managed asset allocation solutions. I believe the success and longevity of the firm reflects the Hellenic values that my parents and community instilled in me. I learned at an early age from my parents and my neighbors how hard people work for the money they earn and because of this, I've always believed that helping others achieve their financial objectives is an honor and a responsibility. Our firm's success is a direct reflection of how well we help each client control risk, preserve capital, and build wealth over the long term.

Once you've achieved success, it's important to give back. Philanthropy is a significant focus for me, and I am especially passionate about tying my philanthropic efforts to education and the Hellenic community. I established endowed chairs in finance and philosophy at my alma mater, Illinois Tech, where I am also a member of the board of trustees.

Many have asked, why finance and philosophy? Finance classes provided an important foundation for my career, but what's special about college is that you have a rare opportunity to learn about a variety of subjects. I encourage students to take philosophy classes—or more classes if they've already taken some. Learning about the many Greek philosophers, especially Plato and Socrates, taught me a great deal about life and gave me historical perspective going back thousands of years.

I credit my study of philosophy with my ability to think critically, to question, and to be innovative. Philosophy helps tie together different disciplines, allowing you to see the big picture. In college, I learned economics is not a math problem. It is economic philosophy: "How are we organized as a society?"

I took on the role of chairman of the National Hellenic Museum in Chicago 10 years ago, initially as a way to honor my parents and our heritage. It is the mission of the museum to share the legacy of Hellenism, to preserve the stories of Greek immigrants and Americans of Greek heritage, and to honor their contributions to the United States. We offer a rich slate of programs that acquaint children and visitors of all backgrounds with Greek history and culture. We strive to provide a foundation, remember our heritage, and motivate future generations.

Preserving our proud history and sharing it with future generations is extremely important to me. I take great pride in my heritage and how it has guided my life journey.

John Catsimatidis, President, Chairman, and CEO of Red Apple Group with subsidiaries in Petroleum, Real Estate, and the Food Industry

My father's example of *philotimo* inspired all aspects of my life, both personal and professional. I learned from his conduct the importance of hard work, love of family, and love of the family name. My father worked tirelessly and sacrificed himself to better others his entire life. For 17 years, he worked night and day on a lighthouse in order to earn a few lire to take care of his three sisters and his mother in the old country. He came to America in 1949, when I was just six months old, and worked seven days a week so he wouldn't have to ask his brothers for any financial support. Growing up, he taught me through his incredible work ethic, the importance and honor of family, character, and self-sufficiency. It served me well.

Philip Christopher, President, CEO, and Founder of American Network Solutions; Founder and President of the Pancyprian Association of America and PSEKA (International Coordinating Committee-Justice for Cyprus)

I was born in Kyrenia, Cyprus, and perhaps our extraordinary power is due to the following: since the Bronze Age in the second and first millennium BC, the Mycenaeans and Achaean Greeks came to Cyprus, bringing their Greek culture with them. From then until today, Greek Cypriots have been in a struggle to maintain their Greek language and Greek culture. How does someone explain that an island that was constantly invaded and occupied by foreigners managed to maintain the Greek language, Greek culture, and the Hellenic values? There is no question that it's due to the extraordinary power of the Greek people, a power that comes from perseverance, courage, determination, and sacrifice. A special power that can be described in one word, *philotimo*. In the Greek culture, *philotimo* is the key to success! It is the secret ingredient to our success.

Congressman Charlie Crist, Member of Congress and Former Governor

I've always believed that it matters where a person comes from. We are all, in part, products of our upbringings and environments. That's why I still like to ask people when I first meet them, "Where ya from?" And for me, that answer starts with my grandfather Adam Christodoulos.

Adam immigrated to America from Cyprus in 1912, coming through Ellis Island. His story, and mine, is the only-in-America kind. He found work shining shoes and then when World War I broke out, he joined the army. When he came back, he married my grandmother, Mary Khoury, whose people were of Lebanese descent. They raised seven children, including my father, with values I still carry with me today—that if you work hard, follow the golden rule, and serve others, anything is possible.

It's with those same values I've been humbled and honored to serve as the governor, attorney general, education commissioner, and now a congressman in the third largest state in the United States—Florida.

Antonis Diamataris, Former Publisher and Editor of *Ethnikos Kirix*; Former Deputy Foreign Minister of Greece for Greeks Abroad

Our Greek Beach, on the Long Island Sound

For decades I would go to work and usually return home late at night. I rarely had time to enjoy our neighborhood and explore its surroundings. I probably have not used the bicycle I bought for that very purpose more than a handful of times.

Thus, when the coronavirus hit us and a lockdown was ordered, I, like almost everyone else, lucky to have a job, started working from home.

For a time, it was great. It was a relief not to have to drive to work and get stuck in traffic—sometimes for an hour and a half each way, sometimes longer. It was great to eat dinner at home, along with my family, since going out to dinner was out of the question—not that any restaurants were open. I discovered our garden and tried my hands on planting some vegetables and trimming some trees, all unsuccessfully. I used the extra time I was saving from commuting by putting my home office in order: by placing all these books that were on the floor or in some random order on the shelves and putting them in some logical order. Not an easy task.

I also started to read those books I had set aside for another time, for another day, when I would "have more time" (as I kept telling myself), but that time had not come for years. I could not possibly imagine that it would be a pandemic that would afford me the extra time. And yet, here it was.

So, I started reading much more than before. And being that reading is my passion, that was great.

The newspaper profession, which I am in, like any other, suffered a lot. Since businesses were closed and employees would not go to work, many newsstands shut down. Thus, hard copy sales were reduced drastically.

And since businesses were shut down and gatherings of more than a few people were prohibited, there were no organizations' activities, and thus, no advertising. It was scary. The good thing was that the online subscriptions skyrocketed. But that could not make up the difference of the loss of the printed editions.

Had the government not stepped in with the PPP loans, it might have been impossible for us to continue as before.

It was the middle of May 2020 when one early afternoon with the sun shining—making everything more beautiful and more reassuring—my wife and I decided to go for a drive, to explore the area.

Frankly, we were tired of staying at home.

So, we got into the car and drove around until we ended up close to the beach in Oyster Bay.

It was not the first time that we passed by that beautiful road which kissed the (usually) tranquil sea, protected from the winds by the shores of Connecticut just across.

We had set down on the sand a few times before, throwing little rocks on the waves and watching the seagulls play and dive into the water for food, grabbing fish and gulping them down.

It was relaxing even though the water was not that clean.

This water had no comparison to the crystal waters of Lemnos, my home island, or my wife's, Crete.

And yet, this time, it looked different. Quite different. Much more inviting. More Greek-like.

We parked the car and started walking on the beach. We walked for a long time. We went all the way down where the boats—small and large—were docked and saw a number of people fishing from the beach.

The ancient tradition of rod fishing that we were so familiar with from Greece was practiced in full swing—mostly from immigrants from Latin American countries. All were wearing masks.

Now the sun was setting. Beautiful, brilliant colors were painting the sky, one of the wonders of the world if you were to ask me.

We stopped there, listening to the sweet sound of the waves breaking on the shore, holding hands, reminiscent of another time and another place—our homeland where the worries of the world had not reached it yet.

So, for us, we discovered a COVID-19 "vaccine" in May of 2020—way before it was developed by scientists. It was a place we could go and find peace of mind and the reassurance that one day, for sure one day, life would go back to what it was. And so we kept going back again and again and yet again.

We went back to our Greek beach, on Long Island, for sanity, for normalcy.

Arthur Dimopoulos, Executive Director of National Hellenic Society

I cannot teach anybody anything. I can only make them think. Socrates, 469–399 BC

The National Hellenic Society (NHS) was established by Greek American leaders, visionaries, and philanthropists who celebrate, preserve, and pass on Hellenic heritage, especially to the next generation. In my leadership role, it is a privilege to have the opportunity to serve as a mentor to a number of student participants in NHS's programs including the NHS's signature program: Heritage Greece.

Heritage Greece is a gift from the NHS to high Greek American academic achievers wishing to reconnect with their respective heritage, culture, roots, and Greek identity. The program is an educational, cultural, and social immersion experience shared with students from the American College of Greece, and as of this summer, also with students from the American College of Thessaloniki/Anatolia College. NHS has sponsored 600+ students on this life-changing program and hopes to expand the number exponentially in the years ahead. The ancient theme of *paideia* guides the NHS as we continue to provide mentorship and career advancement guidance and programs to alumni of the Heritage Greece program.

Socrates' admonition should give us pause to reflect on the role and importance of critical thinking. My humble insight and advice to students is to dispel them of the notion of the popular adage: it's not what you know, it's who you know. I posit what one knows, determines who one is, therefore, what one knows, determines who you know in this life and tempers the depth and quality of the relationships one establishes.

A winding river ebbing through the desert provides sustenance and life to the surrounding riverbanks and the creatures nestled nearby are nurtured by the life-giving water. Like the river, learning, education, and the passion for knowledge is manna and sustenance for body, mind, soul, and the heart. Over eons of time, the river cuts through even the hardest of stone leaving its mark for generations to admire. The fruits borne of ideas and the actions giving them form and substance are the marks we leave behind. A passion to know, wonder, and guide others is the pathway to excellence. This legacy of critical thinking as shaped by our ancient forebears shall continue to bind us from generation to generation.

Michael Dukakis, Former Governor and Nominee for President of the US

Ever since I got interested in politics—and that started when I was nine or ten years of age—I have been proud to be a Greek American politician. Some of that involved our history as a people who believed in and practiced politics. Some of it had to do with the fact that I was a kid during the Nazi occupation of Greece during World War II and tales of the bravery of the Greek Resistance which we learned from our relatives in Greece.

But much of it was the story of my parents and, like so many Greek immigrants, what they were able to contribute to their adopted country when they arrived here as young immigrants. My dad was 15 and grew up in Asia Minor. He decided in 1912 he wanted to come to America to get an education and settled like so many Greek immigrants in Lowell, Massachusetts. He worked in the mills. He worked in restaurants. But he came here to get an education, and 12 years after he arrived at Ellis Island, he was graduating from the Harvard Medical School. How he did it is a remarkable story of its own, but he was one of the first Greek-speaking doctors in New England and practiced medicine in Boston for over 50 years.

My mother came here with her family from Larissa when she was nine and settled with them in Haverhill, Massachusetts. Thanks to an elementary school principal in Haverhill named Stanley Gray, she not only graduated from high school but went on to college at Bates in Maine and graduated Phi Beta Kappa in 1925. She was one of the first Greek immigrant girls to go to college and graduate with honors.

So, with parents like them, you can understand the kind of pride I grew up with in them and their achievements. And it didn't take long to begin to realize that I was part of an ethnic group that was contributing much to its adopted country with hard work, a strong desire to support their children's education, and pride in who they were and the contributions they could make to their adopted country.

In fact, any Greek American who decides to seek public office begins with the advantage of being part of a heritage that is widely admired and respected. But it also requires us to help our fellow

Americans understand just how important immigrants have been and continue to be to our country and its future. That is something we should never forget—not just as Greeks but as part of the remarkable story of America and its achievements—the result in so many cases of the contributions of immigrants from every corner of the globe.

Peter Economides, Founder of Felix BNI

I left home at the age of sixteen.
But I never left home ...

I left my family behind at the age of twenty-seven.
But I never left my family behind ...

When I think back on my life I realise that this is how I gained strength.
I was always free.
But I was never alone.

I have always had a Big Greek Family with me.
My mother and my father.
My brother and sister.
My nephew and nieces.
My aunts and uncles.
My cousins.
My Yiayia and Papou.

They were always at my side.
Talking to me.
Listening to me.
Connecting with me.
Trusting me.
Loving me.
Encouraging me.
Inspiring me.
But most of all, knowing and understanding me.

I grew up in Johannesburg.
My parents were both born in South Africa.
Mom's parents were refugees from the island of Imbros who fled in 1922.
Dad's parents were from Larissa.
They came to South Africa sometime around 1915, in search of a better life.

I have often marvelled at the courage and self-confidence of my remarkable ancestors. Imagine embarking on a one-way journey to the southernmost tip of Africa without being able to Google the weather—nor anything else for that matter. Wow!

But they did it.

They survived.

And they thrived.

I did pretty well at school.

Despite the fact that my parents never—not even once—asked whether I had done my homework. They just assumed that I would do it. Or—at least do enough of it to get by.

I did well enough to skip an entire year of school.

Which meant that I went to university at the age of sixteen.

I went to university in Cape Town, 1.000 miles away from home.

I returned to Johannesburg four years later with an honours degree in business.

Following a compulsory period in the army, I followed the unspoken plan and started working at Dad's very successful heavy manufacturing firm, something he'd started up in our back garden when I was a little kid.

I was enjoying all of this but was feeling itchy …

I spoke to Dad.

"Dad, this is not what I want to do."

"What do you want to do?" he asked.

"I want to be a big deal on Madison Avenue."

"Where the hell is that?"

I explained.

He looked at me with a huge smile on his face and said, "Show them who we are."

And this is how my global adventure began.

I joined McCann-Erickson in Johannesburg, a subsidiary of the McCann-Erickson Worldwide Advertising Agency headquartered in New York.

A few years later they sent me to Hong Kong as regional account director.

One day I received a call from someone at McCann-Erickson in New York.

"You're Greek aren't you?"

"Yes," I replied.

"Do you speak Greek?"

"Yes," I lied.

I learnt Greek as chief executive officer in Greece. And later I learnt Spanish as chief executive officer in Mexico and senior vice president for Latin America.

Finally—12 years after leaving South Africa—I became a big deal on Madison Avenue. I was appointed as executive vice president, worldwide director of client services at McCann-Erickson Worldwide, the world's largest global advertising agency.

A few years later I left McCann-Erickson to join TBWA\Worldwide, the famous ad agency founded by Bill Tragos, a Greek American with roots in Kalamata. It is here that I met Steve Jobs when we worked on the relaunch of Apple in 1997.

I had done it.

But I felt the itch ...

Only this time it was a Greek itch.

So, in 1999 I packed up and returned to my beloved Greece.

And that's where I've been ever since.

Living with the Greeks.

Working with the world.

Thanks to my Big Greek Family.

You are always at my side.

Talking to me.

Listening to me.

Connecting with me.

Trusting me.

Loving me.

Encouraging me.

Inspiring me.

But most of all, knowing and understanding me.

I feel free.

But I never feel alone.

Mike Emanuel, Chief Washington Correspondent, Fox News

My Greek heritage is central to who I am today. From birth, core principles were drilled into us—family, faith, and relentless work ethic. There were stories told of what our grandparents sacrificed for us to be here with limitless opportunities. My grandparents' generation emphasized to my parents the critical importance of education leading to endless opportunities in this great country. My parents shared with their three sons the tremendous challenges their parents faced coming to a country where they did not speak the language. But they were determined to make it here, so their children and future generations could live the American Dream.

As a child, we lived walking distance from the Holy Trinity Greek Orthodox Church in Westfield, New Jersey, so I could walk to attend services, Greek school, Greek dance practice, and youth group meetings. My parents drove the three of us much of the time, but we were close enough that I could just go there on my own too. That was our culture, and the center of my family's community. My childhood priest, Father Alexander Leondis, taught us to love Christ, and equipped us for life in a challenging world. Our friends in that community became extended family, who helped guide us as we were growing up.

My dream was to get into the television news business. My civil engineer father and Wall Street mother encouraged me to chase my dream. The first place to offer me an on-air position was the ABC affiliate in Midland-Odessa, Texas. As someone who was a shy child, I knew I was not the most natural broadcaster. For one, I had to get comfortable being on live television. But I was determined I would be relentless in polishing my skills and would work tirelessly to make the most of my opportunities.

It was a real test since I didn't know anyone in Texas, and the closest Greek Orthodox churches were two hours away in Lubbock and San Angelo, so I was leaving the security blanket of my community. Plus, when you are the new person in a TV newsroom, you get to work all of the holidays. Missing Christmas, Easter, Thanksgiving, and other family gatherings wasn't easy, but I loved the work.

In subsequent jobs in Waco and Austin, Texas; Los Angeles; and

Dallas; there were Greek Orthodox churches. Those communities welcomed me with open arms, which was comforting being a long distance from my close-knit family in New Jersey.

Years later, when I covered the White House during the Bush 43 and Obama years, I frequently thought of the conversations I wish I could have had with my immigrant grandparents. I was so blessed to have the opportunity to ask questions of Presidents George W. Bush and Barack Obama in the Oval Office. I did one-on-one interviews with President Bush and Vice President Cheney. President Obama called on me to ask questions at numerous news conferences. I had the opportunity to travel the world with both leaders on Air Force One. I also did thousands of live reports on Fox from the White House North Lawn.

I tried to picture the faces of my grandparents, who sacrificed it all for these kinds of opportunities. Would they have ever dreamed that their grandson would be in the Oval Office, on Air Force One, and attending White House events? I feel such gratitude to them for giving us the American Dream.

After the September 11th attacks, I was also asked by my bosses to become a war correspondent. I made multiple tours of Afghanistan on assignment and embedded with US Army 10th Mountain Division soldiers in Iraq. I made the decision to bring my faith with me. I wore my gold cross around my neck, carried an icon in my jacket pocket, and had icons with me in my hotel room, in military housing, or even when we slept on the roof of a Baghdad police station. Our Greek Orthodox faith sustained me in the difficult days after 9/11, and over the past 20 years as I traveled to hot spots around the globe.

Maria Foscarinis, Esq., Founder, National Homelessness Law Center

There is no question that my Greek heritage has been critical to my career and life. A confluence of factors contributed: a strong sense of family and, from that, of community more broadly; a commitment to keep trying, and to not give up in the face of adversity; and a strong desire to do the right thing, whatever that might be.

I grew up in a Greek home in New York City, but not in a Greek neighborhood, and I was always aware of being different. In my American school, with my American friends, I was "the Greek," the one with the funny last name, the one whose parents had a foreign accent. The one who spoke a different language at home.

Even though my parents were both fluent in English, they insisted that we always speak Greek together. They loved and appreciated the Greek language, and they wanted to make sure I was fluent in it. I didn't go to Greek school; my father gave me lessons in grammar himself in the evenings, something I did not always enjoy or appreciate then, though now I am glad that I am fluent.

Every summer when my American friends and classmates went to summer camp or vacation homes I went to Greece with my parents, where most of my family still lived. During the winter I worked on improving my Greek so I could write letters to my uncles, aunts, and cousins in Greece. It took me a year but at age 12 I read my first complete book in Greek; it was a beautiful one by Menelaos Loudemis, about a Greek boy who gazed up at the sky and counted the stars.

Growing up in a Greek home opened up the world for me. It showed me that there is not just one way to speak, to write, to eat, to be with other people—there are many. It also helped me see that not everyone had what I had.

When I first started going to Greece there were still villages without electricity or running water, where people lived much more precariously than I did in our apartment on the Upper East Side of Manhattan. Not always, but sometimes there was also hardship; much of what I took for granted was simply not available. While I didn't have to travel but a few blocks from home to realize my privilege, in my case the realization came first and most intimately during those family trips to Greece.

The most salient influence though were the stories I heard from my parents almost nightly at the dinner table about the suffering and deprivation they experienced during the German occupation of Greece. Even though food was plentiful in the countryside, the wartime disruption of transportation meant food could not get to the cities. In Athens, every morning the corpses of those who had died of starvation overnight would be swept from the streets. My mother was there then, studying medicine, and her skin darkened from malnutrition.

But they also told stories of courageous resistance in the face of oppression, often at great personal risk and sacrifice, and these stories inspired me. They suffered tremendously and experienced terrible losses, but they fought for a better, more just, and humane world. These stories painted a vision of a world beyond individual self-interest but rather collective good.

The stories resonated with a pervasive aspect of Greek culture: a sense of the community, a desire to help and care for others, an instinct for hospitality or *philoxenia*. The idea that we are all connected, and that we each have an obligation to our fellow human beings. And the conviction that we must also act on that obligation.

There are many different ways to do so. My particular interest was always to find a way to take action to fight poverty here in the US, which I consider unacceptable in a country as wealthy as ours. That's what led me to go to law school, in hope of acquiring the knowledge and practical tools to take action. Eventually, I started my legal career at a large, Wall Street law firm, where I volunteered to take a pro bono case representing homeless families who had been denied emergency shelter.

Seeing firsthand the dire poverty in which these families were living—in the midst of abundance—and the difference I could make as a young lawyer led me eventually to leave my firm for a different career path as an advocate for this cause. Ultimately, it led me to found in 1989 a nonprofit organization dedicated to using the power of the law to end homelessness in America.

Our organization, the National Homelessness Law Center (formerly known as the National Law Center on Homelessness & Poverty), has made and is making a big impact. We've persuaded Congress to fund housing and social services for millions of people experiencing or at risk of homelessness; we've gone to court to protect the rights of homeless children to go to school, ensuring hundreds of thousands have access to education; we've persuaded cities that punishing people for being homeless is not a solution, and that housing is the way to end homelessness.

Most important, we've never given up in making the case that housing is a basic human right that we all need and deserve. Now, we are making headway as leaders in government are starting to heed our call.

To me this has been a natural extension of caring for others, of being part of a larger community, of fighting for justice, taking action, not giving up. We can call it *philotimo*.

Nicholas Gage, Author and Film Producer

The Greek Legacy

I came to America at the age of nine without knowing a word of English, but by the time I was a senior in college, I had won a national award for the best published writing by a college student sponsored by the Hearst Foundation and it was presented to me by President John F. Kennedy at the White House on May 23, 1963.

At a dinner after the presentation, I was sitting next to Randolph Hearst, the head of the foundation, and he asked me who was my favorite writer, and I quickly replied Ernest Hemingway. He said to me, "I like him but there is no writer as great as William Shakespeare. Not only was he eloquent, but he was so profound." And he began to quote some lines from *Hamlet*. "What a piece of work is man, how noble in reason, how infinite in functions, in actions how like an angel, in apprehensions, how like a God."

I smiled at him and said, "That's beautiful but you know Shakespeare stole that whole concept from Sophocles." He said, "What?!" I said, "Yes, he stole that from Sophocles—the famous lines from *Antigone*: "Wonders are many, but none more wondrous than man. He crosses the storm gray sea, plows the earth, subdues the beasts, cures illnesses, conquers all except death."

Mr. Hearst looked at me and then turned away. I thought I made him mad as he started talking to other board members of the foundation. Later in the evening when he announced the awards, he declared that the board had decided to double the first prize from $2,000 to $4,000, which was a tremendous amount of money in those days and allowed me to pay for my graduate school education at Columbia University.

I like to relate this story not to boast, or maybe a little to boast, but to make the point that it always pays to be proud of your heritage.

And who has a greater heritage than we Greeks? Yet we have little of that legacy left. The monuments are fallen into ruin, the sculptures broken and defaced, the writings few and fragmented but the bits and pieces are enough. They challenge and inspire like little else man has achieved. From those broken columns we can see that no edifice can match the Parthenon or the Aghia Sofia. From the bits of pieces of sculpture, we know that no modern artist can stand up to Praxiteles or Phidias. The few extant dramas of Aeschylus, Sophocles, Euripides can be matched in power only by Shakespeare. No poet can touch Sappho or Hesiod. Outside the Bible, no prose can equal Plato, whose intellect, moreover, was so encompassing that they render all other philosophical insights into mere footnotes, as Lord Whitehead observed.

The foundations of what we value most in the West were laid down by the Greeks, foundations so strong that they have supported the whole structure of our civilization for 25 centuries.

The most important of those values is the right to live under one's own control and not another's, in a word, freedom. When human beings began gathering in communities, they quickly concluded that societies could not endure very long without order, but it was always believed that order could not be achieved without authoritarian rule. All of the previous societies before the Greeks—the Egyptians, the Assyrians, the Hebrews, the Chinese—they were all tyrannies. The Greeks were the first people to make the great leap of faith in human nature and believe that it was possible to have both order and freedom, and it is on that principle that most of the world functions today.

There is another value that the Greeks bequeathed the world. In comparing previous civilizations to the Greeks, the noted classicist Edith Hamilton observed that all were preoccupied with death and focused all their art on death while the Greeks turned full-faced to life. "To rejoice in life," she wrote, "to find the world beautiful and exciting, distinguished Greeks from all those who came before."

The contributions of Greeks to Western civilization continued a thousand years after Athens became a backwater of the Roman Empire through the works of Euclid, Archimedes, Xeno, Plutarch, and many more. Christianity was spread through the Roman Empire and the West by Greeks. St. Paul preached in Greek and the Gospels were all written in Greek. When power in the Roman Empire shifted to Byzantium, its administration remained Roman but its language and culture became Greek. After the Fall of Constantinople in 1453, thousands of Byzantine artists and scholars fled to Italy and

became catalysts for the Renaissance, which was fueled by passion for Hellenic art, literature, and philosophy. As the Renaissance spread through Northern Europe, Greek legends, images, and ideals captured the imagination of writers, artists and thinkers including Shakespeare, Jefferson, Byron, Yeats, and Tolstoy, who began learning Greek at 42. "Without knowledge of Greek," he wrote, "there is no education."

The thousands of Greeks who fled to this country in the last century, escaping poverty, war, famine, and persecution, were not poets or philosophers. For the most part, they were uneducated refugees eager to do whatever work they could find, immigrant men living crowded together in squalid rooms until they could bring over a brother, a cousin, a wife, or a child. But no matter how uneducated a Greek or how menial his work, he usually applied himself with the same determination to excel as his ancestors.

The Greeks' eagerness to work for poor wages and their quick success created a groundswell of prejudice against them, early in the last century. During the interim before and after World War I, Greeks were characterized in the American newspapers as the scum of the earth, a vicious element unfit for citizenship, and ignorant, depraved, and brutal foreigners. The worst incidents against Greek immigrants took place in Omaha, Nebraska, early in the last century. On the outskirts of the city, a shantytown developed of several thousand Greek laborers, mostly railroad workers, and they were not liked by the local citizens who considered them less than white. Then on February 19, 1909, a policeman saw one of the laborers walking with a local woman and became enraged and attacked the man, who killed the cop during the fight that ensued. Local officials whipped the townspeople into a frenzy, yelling, "One drop of American blood is worth all the Greek blood in the world!" The mob then ravaged through the Greek quarter burning almost all of it to the ground, destroying 36 businesses and driving all Greeks from the city. Yet today, Greek Americans in Omaha are as highly respected as any ethnic group in the region.

But such respect was hard won in Omaha and everywhere else in America by our parents and grandparents and we can never forget what they bequeathed us. Greeks were the last European immigrants to settle in America, but in the short time we have been here, we have achieved the highest education level of any ethnic group and the second highest per capita income. But we have worked hard to not only become successful, but also to win the respect and approval for who we are and what we do.

The ancient Greeks defined happiness as the exercise of vital powers along the lines of excellence affording them scope. Greeks have pursued such happiness in America vigorously and America has given us the scope to do it. In our emphasis on achievement, we have followed the lead of our new country, and in our attachment to family and friends, we have held to the traditions of the old. In so doing, I think we have chosen the best of both worlds.

The reality of America proved harsh for the uneducated Greek immigrants who came to the United States, but they suffered gladly because they knew that their labors would give their children the chance to fulfill their dreams. Pericles said about the ancient Greeks, "The memory of our achievements will be bequeathed to posterity forever." Greeks in America are still making impressive contributions to that bequest.

The achievements of famous modern Greeks like Maria Callas and Aristotle Onassis that I describe in my book *Greek Fire*, the struggles of immigrants like my father, Cristos Gtazoyiannis, that I recount in *A Place for Us*, and the sacrifices of women like my mother that I portray in *Eleni*, are all part of the tapestry that illustrates the history of Modern Greeks. In these books, I tried to bear witness to what they have contributed to who we are as a people and what the Nobel prize winning poet Odysseas Elytis meant when he wrote:

And let them say that we walk with
our heads in the clouds—
Those who have never felt, my friend,
With what iron, what stones,
what blood, what fire,
We build, dream and sing.

(adapted from 2013 speech to GOYA/YAL conference)

John Georges, Chairman and CEO of Georges Enterprises

Hellenism has been one of the biggest influences in my entire life. After my father settled down in the United States, he constantly reminded my family of our roots. During my childhood summers, my parents would send my siblings and me to Greece to live in the village. We developed a phenomenal bond not only with our cousins, but also with the country itself. Growing up in New Orleans, I, like all Greek kids, was an altar boy in Church and worked the Greek Festival every year at a young age. When I started work at the family business, my father and uncle instilled in me the values they learned from my grandfather—who started the company a few years after emigrating from Greece in the 1910s. Being Greek is in our DNA and regardless of where we live or how we grew up we all share the same characteristics with Greeks around the globe. My children are third generation Greek Americans and yet maintain Greek heritage and traditions.

New Orleans is the first and oldest Greek church and community in America. Also New Orleans had the first and oldest Greek consulate in America due to shipping interests. As well, Tulane University and LSU were full of visiting professors from Greece. Frequently, visiting Greeks would attend church and my parents would host them for Sunday lunch. Like many Greeks, growing up in the church and community and knowing dozens of diplomats, has had a profound influence on me that I have passed onto my children.

Theodora (Sideropoulos) Hancock, Lt. Colonel (retired) USAF; Founder and President of the Hellenic American Women's Council

When I informed my father that I was considering joining the US Air Force as an officer, he asked in Greek, *"and they will take you?"* *"Yes Dad, they are recruiting me."* He literally grew taller in his chair.

As a child, he was a refugee from the Pontos area, hardly finished elementary school, fought in WWII and the subsequent civil war in Greece as an enlisted man, and he was a wounded warrior. In middle age, he immigrated to the US. His English was limited. And now, his young daughter was going to be an officer in the United States Air Force— only in America.

At the time, I had not realized the depth of his pride. I do now!

My parents highly valued education and ensured we were educated. However, they never tried to influence my career choices. They instilled in me self-worth and confidence. Being of Greek heritage was a source of great pride. One of his favorite sayings was, *"When our ancestors discovered philosophy, the sciences, and built the Parthenon, the rest of the world was still climbing trees."*

This gave me pride in my heritage and self-confidence. I always felt I could do anything—be anything. If I did not know how to do something, I could learn. If anyone else could do it, so could I. Just tell me what the mission is and I'll get it done. After all, I was Greek!

My parents never spoke of hard work—they demonstrated it. They spoke Greek at home—actually Pontian Greek. They also demonstrated strong faith, service to the community, and leadership. *"Do it, don't talk about it."* I carry these values to this day.

My Greek heritage continues to influence every aspect of my life.

Kelly Vlahakis-Hanks, President and CEO of ECOS

My Greek heritage has been a deep and powerful thread woven through my life. From the profound influence of my Greek father to the unwavering support of my extended Greek family to the values of Hellenic culture I hold dear, my Greek heritage has shown me a path to success in life that I'm deeply grateful for.

I first developed my love for Greece as a young child traveling with my father to Crete every summer. I listened to his firsthand accounts of surviving Nazi occupation and civil war and was fascinated by the stories of resilience and pride. My love of the planet came from my father, as I enjoyed the natural beauty of Greece with him and swam with him in the Cretan and Libyan Seas.

When I moved to Los Angeles to go to UCLA, I was immediately embraced by the Greek community there, and it was there at the Hellenic American Students Organization that I honed my leadership and public speaking skills and strengthened my commitment to democracy, justice, and peace. I went on to lead the American Hellenic Council in Los Angeles, and my love of country and homeland was a very motivating factor as I helped inform the American public and the government on issues of democracy, human rights, peace, and stability in Southern Europe and the Eastern Mediterranean, with an emphasis on Greece and Cyprus.

Our company ECOS—founded by my father Van Vlahakis over 50 years ago—was inspired by Greece and his homeland of Crete. *Ecos* is Greek for home, and today ECOS helps keep homes clean and families safe with cleaning products inspired by nature. Home and family are so central to Greek culture, and the foundation of "family first" has been a guiding light for me both personally and professionally, and today, I am proud to helm our company as we achieve unprecedented milestones in sustainability and green chemistry. ECOS was the first company in the world to achieve carbon neutrality, water neutrality, and TRUE Platinum Zero Waste certification at our US facilities, and now we are a Climate Positive company, restoring 110% of our impact to the planet.

A Greek family is so much more than parents and children—it's a great extended family of aunts and uncles, grandparents and cousins—first cousins, second cousins, third cousins!—that support one another, lean on one another, and lift one another up. I've had the great fortune of having many family members here in the US as well as in Greece, and I'm proud to have so many wonderful family members in our ECOS operations who have helped us achieve great success.

I'm inspired every day by the principles of Greek culture, of determination and bravery, of respect for nature and appreciation of its beauty, of protection of the ocean and all she gives us. I reflect on these principles every day as I lead ECOS at our facilities across the US and in Greece.

The very first award that I won for my leadership was the "Spirit of Bouboulina" award at UCLA. Laskarina Bouboulina was a Greek naval commander and heroine of the Greek War of Independence in 1821, and she's remembered as a Greek national hero who was critical to gaining their independence. She was a strong woman, a courageous woman—a woman who was unafraid to lead her troops and inspired them to fight for what was right. I hope to honor Laskarina Bouboulina in the way I run our business as a champion for human and planetary wellness, and also in the way I raise my daughter, to lead by example, to show strength, to show her she can do anything she wants to do and be anyone she wants to be.

From the time I was a little girl, I always felt loved, supported, and uplifted by my Greek family and my Greek community, and it was that love and support that gave me the strength and conviction to find success. It's the Greek values that I have stood upon, the values I hold dear to lead a purpose-driven life. It's the Greek values—courage, kindness, generosity, *philotimo*—that have been the foundation of my success. I am deeply grateful for my Greek heritage, and I am incredibly proud to be a Greek American.

Menas C. Kafatos, Fletcher Jones Endowed Chair Professor of Computational Physics at Chapman University and Director of the Center of Excellence in Earth Systems Modeling and Observations (CEESMO)

"Philotimo, the Philosophy of Life"

I was born and raised in Irakleion, in the beautiful island of Crete, Greece. My parents, Constantine and Helen Kafatos, instilled in me from an early age the value of truthfulness, honor, humility, and following one's dreams. They were learned people and although not wealthy, they had plenty of wealth in traditions and good behavior. My father associated with the intelligentsia of Irakleion, he personally knew Nikos Kazantzakis, was a friend of Lefteris Alexiou and his son Stelios Alexiou, director of the Archaeological Museum, the painter Thomas Fanourakis, members of the church, and others. Eventually my father became a student of Fr. Paisios. My mother was niece of writer Pantelis Prevelakis of Rethymnon. My father reached the highest civil service in the Department of Agriculture as *epitheoritis* (inspector) of agriculture of Crete. My uncle George Xiroudakis, brother of my mother, was a renowned mathematician in Crete and director of the Korais Lyceum, founded by Eleftherios Venizelos. My father and mother instilled in me the love of art, philosophy, and literature while my uncle the love of mathematics which led to love for science.

The immediate Kafatos family followed the value of *philotimo* and made sure that it was an integral part of our upbringing for my two brothers, Antonis and Fotis, and myself. As I was growing up, I noticed that when one "gives one's word," it is better than any contract. As part of their *philotimo*, my father never borrowed money, insisting that we have to live within our means. My mother, likewise, followed the traditions of the Orthodox Church and her uncle was the metropolitan of Crete Evmenios. Although at the time playing cards was a favored activity of many middle-class women, she never played cards. Among other things, my brothers and I never smoked for which we are grateful as never having to face getting out of this habit. Among the top characteristics of *philotimo*, was telling the truth, working hard, honoring the elders, and being a true friend.

Constantine Kafatos was born in the village of Monastiraki, near the town of Amari, Prefecture of Rethymnon, while my mother, Helen Xiroudaki, her family originally from Sfakia, was born and raised in Rethymnon. He emigrated to America in 1914, hardly 14 years old, not knowing a single word of English. He made it to New York City, their merchant ship almost sunk by a German U-boat in the Atlantic. He stayed in the States, excelled in education, which was hard at the time, and even attended Cornell for a few years. He learned the values of American society, became a citizen and worked hard, earning an honest living. He told us that for him *philotimo* was very practical; when faced with a decision, he would always ask himself, "What would my father do?" and he said that always kept him on the right path, away from temptations and dubious life that many immigrants had to face. Eventually he decided after 14 years to return to Greece, where he was introduced by a common friend to my mother and they got married in the mid-thirties. They moved to Irakleion where my father entered the agricultural service. My two brothers were born before World War II. When the Nazis invaded Greece, they were all caught in the effects of the war. Although Constantine was always a man of peace, right after the Battle of Crete, he was almost executed by the Germans as he knew English, had been an American citizen, and they suspected a friend of the Americans and the English, all of course being true. He was saved at one point by an Austrian teacher who took his name off a list of leaders and members of the intelligentsia to be executed. My parents and my brothers lived in the village of Fortetsa outside Irakleion where it was relatively safer, easier to have food—bread, vegetables, and goat's milk were plentiful—and raise their young children.

I was lucky to have been born after the war. For me *philotimo* was to work hard at school, learn and read all the time. I lived in the world of history, read ancient works and developed a love for mathematics from my uncle George. From a very young age, I was drawing and painting so it was always assumed by everyone that I would go to Paris to study fine arts at the Sorbonne. However, at the age of 14, I decided to make a leap: I told my father art is so natural to me, I want to do something else. He asked me what. I replied science. Without hesitating he said, "Then you have to go to America."

The magic of the dark skies in Crete, away from city lights, gave me a sense of universality. Perhaps the sense of origin of *philotimo*? I remember gazing at the night sky at the Milky Way and wondering what is out there. I decided to become an astronomer. My brother Fotis had already gone to Cornell University where he studied biology and then to Harvard where he became the youngest professor to be granted tenure. He sent me a three-inch reflector and I used it many nights observing the planets, nebulae, and the moon with my uncle George and my cousins. I took all the exams and entered Cornell. I remember leaving Piraeus in the summer of 1963 on the ocean liner *Queen Frederika* and wondering what would wait for me in America.

Following the value of *philotimo* which translates for us intellectuals as working hard, doing honest work, and advancing following humanist values, I graduated with honors from Cornell in physics and went to MIT for my doctoral studies. I had met Philip Morrison at Cornell and when he moved to MIT, after I became accepted there, he and I decided to work together. Morrison was a brilliant physicist and a pioneer in astrophysics. Actually he was a student of J. Robert Oppenheimer, and worked on the Manhattan Project, the building of the atomic bomb. Phil, after he witnessed firsthand the destruction that befell Hiroshima, became an ardent pacifist and against the hydrogen bomb. Although he did not know the word *philotimo*, he certainly applied it to his life: honest science, working for humanity, and being responsible for his students.

Today, after so many years, I can say that whatever I have achieved is due to previous generations, hard work, and not wishing anything negative for anyone. Having studied quantum mechanics and astrophysics, I now work extensively on the implications of quantum mechanics, the role of the mind in our views of reality and firmly believe what John A. Wheeler, protégé of Einstein, said, "We live in a participatory universe." Today I turn more and more to philosophy, which I actually always loved. Philosophy and philotimo

I feel are twins: the love of wisdom leads to love of honor and vice versa. Moreover, and most important, science and spirituality are actually closely related to each other: one cannot but lead to spiritual understanding when observing the vast universe. Spirituality which actually was a strong tenet of both my parents, is now leading me to introspection and meditation, studying the Platonists, mystical Christianity, Buddhism, and Indian traditions of non-duality, to name a few. In our age of division and strife, it is my duty to give a different perspective to the youth, coming directly from science and philosophy. That is my philosophy of life and *philotimo*. Today I do a lot of writing, giving seminars and I feel the values of the ancients continue through me as I also tried to instill the same to my three sons. Most importantly, perhaps all the young people are in a sense my sons and daughters and these days as the coronavirus is forcing us all inside our homes, we actually reach out to each other through technology. Having married Susan Yang, a Korean American, a neuroscientist and computational expert, I look at the similarities of these two countries at opposite sides of the earth—Greece and Korea—and the United States where so many of us have made our home and moving together forward. Having visited so many different countries, I find, like Kazantzakis, that universal values bind us together. Divisions are the product of the erroneous mind attached to the ego, whether individual or national. We cannot afford that anymore as humanity. Although a scientist of Hellenic origin, I value traditions, cultures, and histories of other nations as my own. If it is that humanity will survive into the next century, we have to shed away the falsehood of division. That truth the ancient Hellenes knew and as such spread the light throughout the world. I know that we are all, foremost, humans. Isn't that after all what Socrates said and taught? First human, then Athenian.

Father Alex Karloutsos, Protopresbyter of the Ecumenical Patriarchate

Hellene or Philhellene? I Am Both

As a young boy I was proud of my family's Greek heritage, but was not fully aware that, although my friends' families were not from Greece, they, too, were inheritors of "a way of life" illumined by Hellas, "the Morningstar of the Western World." Knowing oneself and living a life worth living was always Greek at its core, but it was, is, and always will be, a universal truth shared by all human beings throughout time.

I realized later on, like Isocrates (436–338 BC) stated, "the word 'Greek' has come to mean not a nation but a way of life. They are called Hellenes who partake of our culture." Percy Shelley, the great English poet of the 19th century, rightly wrote, "We are all Greeks: our laws, our literature, our religion, our arts have their root in Greece." These insights helped me understand fully that I am not simply a Hellene or Philhellene: proudly I can say, I Am Both.

Being a Greek Orthodox Christian priest is central to my knowledge of self and following Jesus Christ, my Lord and Savior, has blessed me with family and friends who have enriched my life with purpose in the service of others. Toward those two ends, purpose and service, I have found SEVEN GREEK *PHILOS* (friends/loves) that, hopefully, are the ideals I try to live up to 24 hours a day.

PHILOTHEOS: the love of God. It all begins and ends with God, the Alpha and the Omega, the Creator of all things visible and invisible.

PHILANTHROPOS: the love of man. Jesus summed it up as the greatest commandment: Love the Lord your God with all your heart, mind and soul and your neighbor as yourself." Every day, I try to answer Saint John the Evangelist's question, "How can you say you love God Whom you have not seen and hate your neighbor whom you have seen?"

PHILOTIMOS: the love of honor. The Greek Secret which inspires us to live honorably, with dignity and grace, and our inner conscience to avoid evil and foolish ways, which brings shame on one's name, family, and legacy.

PHILOXENOS: the love of stranger. In Ancient Greece, the god Zeus would disguise himself as a stranger. Our forebears always set an extra setting at the table to welcome an unknown guest. Jesus said the same, "I was a stranger and you welcomed me." The exact opposite of xenophobia.

PHILOSOPHOS: the love of wisdom. To love wisdom is to be a perpetual student throughout one's life. Socrates said it best, "The older I grow the more I continue to learn," because "one thing I know is that I know nothing."

PHILOPTOCHOS: the love of the poor. One cannot love God and man, and not feel the pain of those less fortunate. Like our Jewish brethren, I try to do a good deed (Mitzvah) every day by "doing unto others as I would have others do unto me."

PHILOKALOS: the love of beauty and good. I believe it is important to see the beauty and wonder of God's creation every day and to see the wonderful beauty and good in the person of our neighbor. As Sophocles exclaimed, "There are many wonders in our universe, but none more wonderful than man."

Peter Karmanos Jr., Chairman and Co-founder of MadDog Technology; Philanthropist

My Greek heritage is my parents, Peter and Fotene Karamanos, who taught me how special it was to be a Hellene. All that I have accomplished is due to the lessons I learned from their struggles as adolescent immigrants in America.

Jimmy Kokotas, Supreme President of the American Hellenic Educational Progressive Association

Our lives are constantly influenced by family, home, and history. As a first-generation Greek American, I have been blessed to have been immersed in two of the greatest cultures in the world. There are many morals, values, and lessons that have helped shape my life. I'd like to share a few of the most important ones.

Faith in God and the love and hope he provides to me as a Greek Orthodox Christian is the greatest gift of my life. My faith gives me the strength and ability to put things into perspective. Life is a little easier when you know something greater than this world is waiting for you and with God and Christ it is attainable.

The importance of family, and the commitment, dedication, and selflessness of my parents, have also been paramount in my life. To know that my mother and father persevered through so many difficult times with their only goal being a better life for my sister and me is humbling. To experience that kind of love has been invaluable to me, especially during my upbringing. It strengthened my faith in God. I contend that being passionate about things in which you believe, and perseverance, are qualities that are important for success. Victory in life does not always come quickly or easily. However, with these principles, it is always within reach. So many of the challenges we face can only be overcome when we have the passion to fight and the perseverance to keep fighting.

The values and principles I have shared also have been instrumental in Greece's history. Through almost 400 years of Ottoman rule, it was passion and perseverance for faith and family that helped our ancestors survive. It eventually won them their freedom. In 1940, when Greece was faced with an insurmountable enemy, it was their passion for faith, family, and freedom that produced the famous "*oxi*." These are the values that changed the course of the war and ultimately helped save the world. They are also the values that most influenced my life.

Ambassador Tom C. Korologos, Former U.S. Ambassador to Belgium; Former Advisor to Five US Presidents

"He was once an altar boy at the Greek Orthodox Church in Salt Lake City. I know that's hard to believe but it's true."
—*Senator Orrin G. Hatch, R-UT, June 17, 2004.*

That was how I was introduced by Utah's senior senator at the U.S. Senate Foreign Relations Committee hearings for my confirmation to become the U.S. ambassador to Belgium. Much laughter ensued and it set the tone for the rest of the hearings, where Senate Majority Leader Robert C. Byrd (D-WV) and seven additional senators from both sides of the political aisle came to introduce me.

As Senator Hatch and the others graciously highlighted in their presentations, my Greek heritage and the typical and traditional Hellenic customs in Salt Lake City created an invaluable blueprint for future accomplishments.

Not unlike many Greek American homes working in family enterprises the world over, in the early 1940s as a preteen I helped out in my father's bar serving beer to customers—my pay was one or two dollars in tips. This once led to my arrest by the anti-vice squad and I was taken to the Salt Lake Police Station not only for being underage "in a bar" but even for "serving beer." I'm not sure what transpired, but my half-amused and half-annoyed father showed up shortly and I went home.

Everything in my childhood was Greek. Cousins, in-laws, uncles and aunts, grandparents, and multiple Greek neighbor families tended to congregate at the slightest excuse and of course, Greek was the spoken language and Greek heritage the inevitable subject. Consequently, when I went to kindergarten, I had some early difficulty understanding and speaking English, having grown up speaking Greek at home, in the neighborhood, and on the playgrounds.

During my Greek school days—attending Greek classes after regular English school—I recited Greek Independence Day poems, participated in plays proudly wearing my grandfather's *foustenala*, and starred in various depictions of Greek independence and history, making my parents very proud.

Church activities also prevailed. I often recited the Orthodox Creed (the *Pystevo*) at church on Sundays and actively participated in the church choir. Throughout all this I came to know the Orthodox Divine Liturgy almost by heart and often recited it in a whisper along with the priests and cantors. This led to more than one suggestion from my father that I should consider becoming a Greek Orthodox priest.

Through the years I have thought about my parents and the values they passed on to me. Perhaps the most important was their work ethic and their support and encouragement to participate in civic and public organizations. My father was treasurer of the Arcadian Brotherhood, an organization involving diaspora Greek Americans who were from Arcadia in Southern Greece. I also joined the Brotherhood as well as AHEPA, The American Hellenic Institute, the Oxi Foundation, the Greek American Youth Organization (GOYA), and the Greek Orthodox churches in the various cities where my career took me. My bartending days also taught me there is no such thing as clockwatching and that you worked until the job is done. I learned to get there early and leave late. One of my carry-over mantras in later years has been, "Be the first person to meetings, it builds confidence."

My parents and my Greek sense of identity also gave me the inspiration to be as kind and generous as possible. This has applied to family, co-workers, official and business staff in various venues, waiters, delivery persons, even ushers at the ballpark. When I worked on Capitol Hill, one of my favorite groups of people in addition to the ultra-high level political leaders of the Western world, were the security guards around the US Senate chamber. I often gave them baseball tickets and made sure they were included in invitations to big ticket events in which I was involved. Being Greek keeps you humble and maybe some lack of hubris came from so many Greek lyrical tragedies.

My Greek upbringing also formed my political development and helped create my total allegiance and loyalty to the United States. I always stand when *The Star Spangled Banner* is played, be it at personal events or on the radio or TV. My emotional attachment to Greek culture also was a contributing factor. This combination helped guide me through nine years as a senior staffer in the United States Senate, served five presidents of the United States, readily accepted a call to serve for a year (2003) in Iraq, three years (2004–2007) as U.S. ambassador to the Kingdom of Belgium, three terms as chairman of the board of the American College of Greece in Athens, various presidential boards and commissions, and as Washington representative for the Republic of Greece.

And all of this because I didn't take up my sainted father's advice to become a priest.

Eleni Kounalakis, Lt. Governor of California; Former US Ambassador to Hungary

Back in the eighth grade, a fellow student made a presentation to our class. Her name was Janie, and she brought an ornate hand-painted document which established, she explained, that her family had come to the United States on the Mayflower. Naturally, all the kids were very impressed. Several joined in, mentioning that their families had been among the earliest pioneer families in California.

When I went home that afternoon, I felt bad about the conversation. It made me feel small—as if being the daughter of an immigrant, and part of a vibrant but very newly established, thick-accented Greek community, might make me less of an American than the other kids in my class, surely less American than Janie. When I told my dad about what happened, he puffed up. "You tell those kids that you are related to Aristotle, Pericles, and Plato!"

That was many, many years ago and today I represent the State of California as the first woman ever elected lieutenant governor. In my last post, I was the first Greek American woman, and so far the only one, to serve as an American ambassador. In all my endeavors I have drawn strength from my love of country, patriotism, and of course dedication to my Golden State.

I have also drawn strength from my status as the daughter of an immigrant, pursuer of the American Dream and as it happens, from a lifetime of believing that indeed I am a descendant of Aristotle, Pericles, and Plato.

Genetic websites like 23 and Me, or Ancestry, have disclaimers about how far back they really go in terms of determining participants' ethnicity—certainly not 2,500 years. My husband, a Cretan, has pointed out that my second toe is just barely longer than my first, and doesn't stick way out like Greek statues. It's another marker of being a real Greek, according to everyone who has that particular genetic feature, including my husband.

But these things don't matter. It also doesn't matter that my family in Greece was very humble—my *yiayia* never learned to read or write. It doesn't matter that my father came here as a boy with nothing—on a ship that was not named the Mayflower. Or that he started out in the fields of this country as a farmworker. No, if there is one thing that has helped me confidently chart my path to leadership—as an American and Californian—it is the fundamental pride that I feel because I am of Greek heritage.

What makes me most proud?

I am proud that Greece is the Birthplace of Democracy. I am proud that Greece is the cradle of Western civilization, reason, logic, philosophy, math, science, theatre, medicine, and the Olympic Games.

I love that Greek mythology to this day contains some of the most sophisticated, accurate depictions of what it means to be a human being, failures and all. I also love that Greek Orthodoxy represents the elevation of LOVE as the driving principle in life and faith.

I am also proud that in the 20th century, Greece was on the right side of history during all the major history-shaping conflicts—A US ally in World War I and World War II, and after a brutal civil war, on the right side of the Iron Curtain. This is no coincidence, and I believe it speaks to the character of the Greek people.

Philotimo, the love of honor, is a key part of the Greek character, passed from parent to child over generations. Rejection of xenophobia, our openness to newcomers, is also embedded in the Greek character.

And of course, Greece itself. It is the most geographically magnificent and magical place in the world with the best, healthiest food, music, and dancing.

Right now, we are living in unprecedented times, and in a highly unpredictable world. In the context of political upheaval, international instability and the Fourth Industrial Revolution, some of the loftiest questions of life are asked. Who am I? What should I believe? What is my purpose?

I feel fortunate for my family, my children, and all of us who are members of the Greek American community—regardless of what percentage Greek you think you are, or what your toes look like—that we have so much history and culture available to us to help us answer life's tough questions.

I also feel fortunate that when I'm questioning these very things myself, in the never-ending endeavor to Know Thyself, a soak in the Mediterranean Sea, a book of mythology, morning in church, song by Theodorakis or even just a bite of perfectly crisped *tiropita*, helps me find my way, every time.

Stamatios M. Krimigis, Emeritus Head of Space Exploration Sector at Johns Hopkins Applied Physics Laboratory

Chasing the Sun, the Planets, and Beyond

Growing up on the Greek island of Chios in the Aegean, gazing at the sky on clear nights (no light pollution there!) and seeing the "billions and billions of stars" as the late Carl Sagan used to say, one could easily be carried away and wonder about all these points of light up there and dream about the existence of other worlds. Not only that, it was hard to escape the history of intellectual ferment that had taken place just a couple of thousand years ago right around the neighborhood: Homer's Rock—on which legend has it he recited his poems for the locals—was just a mile from our house, and Thales and Euclid and Democritos were roaming the shores of Ionia just across the strait in Asia Minor, and Pythagoras was talking about the theory of numbers and inventing the Pythagorian theorem on the island of Samos just a few miles south of Chios. These people laid the foundations of the scientific, in contrast to the religious, view of nature in our world, and our teachers kept recounting all of this history as if it had happened yesterday. So, the incentive and stimulation for learning was all around, and I became fascinated early on with rocket propulsion—the home-made variety—so we could aim and shoot rockets during the Easter midnight service at the neighboring church's dome, less than a mile away.

But it was my father, an early immigrant to this country, who decided that America was the modern world's Athens and stipulated that I go to college here—so I packed my bags at the age of 18 and flew to Minneapolis in late fall—and I must say I was somewhat surprised that there was a temperature difference between Chios and Minneapolis, from +70°F to well below freezing; I noticed the ground below the airplane was all white—no brown patch was visible anywhere.

The United States of America is a great country. I'm grateful every day that my father chose to become an immigrant in this country a century ago, thus affording me the good fortune of being an American citizen by birth. When I arrived in the US from Chios at the age of 18, my English language skills left a lot to be desired and I had difficulty coping as a freshman physics student at the University of Minnesota. But I was made to feel right at home by fellow students and professors alike, and soon I adapted to the system and embraced it wholeheartedly. At no point did I sense that I was discriminated against—that I was not competing on a level playing field or that others were preferred because I had an accent. And never in my career did I fill out an application to be promoted to some higher-level position; I was happy to do the best job I knew how at the position I had. My supervisors were the ones who insisted that I take on more responsibility. I recall that in 1990, the then director of the Applied Physics Laboratory (APL) of Johns Hopkins, Dr. Carl Bostrom, called me up while I was on Capitol Hill talking to congressional committee staff and informed me that he had just signed a memo to the APL staff appointing me as head of the Space Department. I was somewhat taken aback, as he added that if I did not accept, I should not bother coming back to the Laboratory—he made a compelling argument, so I accepted. My main point is that at no time did I doubt the fairness and decency, and the idealism and promise of America as a great country where meritocracy rules and everyone can make history, because this is what America is all about.

So, the opportunities were there, the educational and social system encouraged hard work, recognition for achievement was given freely, and the motto of my teacher, Prof. James Van Allen (discoverer of the Van Allen Radiation Belt surrounding Earth), was to "give yourself a chance to get lucky." What that means is that if you study hard and pursue excellence in all you do, then when an opportunity arises you will recognize it and grasp it; but if you are unprepared, then you will not even recognize the opportunity. This type of environment was very much in line with the classical Greek saying in Homer "αιέν αριστεύειν," i.e., "pursue excellence" and Socrates' "The unexamined life is not worth living." For me, with this set of values, the path was really laid out: pursuing excellence and working hard was the way to send, with my teams, instruments and spacecraft to every planet in our solar system and beyond. And to complete the job by helping to send the Parker Solar Probe in 2018 on its way to our own star, the sun. It has already passed by the sun six times, and in another couple of years will speed by it at 400,000 miles per hour at a distance of about four million miles. And the external temperature of the heat shield protecting the spacecraft will be about 2500°F (or 1400°C). That is hot!

Niki Leondakis, CEO of CorePower Yoga

I was raised in a small town in Western Massachusetts with just three Greek families in the town, my family being one, my cousins on my mother's side the other, and the superintendent of schools being the third. That the superintendent of schools was a Greek was a great source of pride for my parents. Both my parents, Nick and Vilma (Basiliki) were 100 percent Greek and their families from the island of Crete. My father came to this country when he was 17 with his 19-year-old sister, Anna, to create a new life. My mother was Greek American, born in Springfield, Massachusetts.

Going to Greek school, Sunday school at the St. George's Greek Orthodox Church's parish hall, Greek festivals, and Greek and Cretan dances constantly surrounded by Greeks was a normal part of our life as children. My parents spoke Greek at home, and I must admit we did have a lot of Greek statuary throughout our house. I learned at a young age all that Greeks contributed to Western civilization. But what I learned that has made a difference in my life was about a way of being. A value system based on Greek culture and philosophy was instilled in me, not through lectures or words, but through my parents' and grandmother's actions and the way they lived their lives.

I learned to find joy and a zest for life no matter what was happening in the world. I watched my father and mother throw parties, always with Greek circle dancing through the house as the highlight of the night. The abundance of home-cooked food and Greek desserts my aunts and uncles all contributed to, and the flowing wine and cocktails—usually bartended by my older brother—were a source of amazement. My father was usually in a corner with a twinkle in his eye, telling our guests' fortunes from the remains of the grinds in a Greek coffee cup turned upside down. Unsurprisingly, my dog, Zorba, was always in the middle of all the action.

I learned about the importance of philanthropy through my mother's and grandmother's tireless contributions as members of Philoptochos and the Cretan Ladies Society. My work with Dress for Success worldwide for the past 20 years was the result of my mother's and grandmother's influence. I also learned about hospitality in the truest sense of the word. We rarely had dinner with just our family—people were always invited to join us at the table—whether it was our next-door neighbor, the television repairman, or someone who worked with my father who he thought needed a home-cooked meal.

I remember that my father through his place of work, Stop & Shop supermarkets, held a fashion show in a parking lot to raise money for a local family who lost their home in a fire. When I was growing up, my father and my mother helped my cousins who were still back in Greece come to the US for an education or to find a new life for themselves. These cousins lived with us for extended periods of time while my father helped them find jobs and until they got on their feet in the US.

My grandparents on my mother's side owned a diner in the town we grew up in. I stayed with my grandmother when my parents went back to Greece for month-long visits and couldn't take all five of us kids with them. They took the older kids on a trip, then the younger kids—each time leaving the ones who stayed behind with our relatives. I loved staying with my grandmother. I learned so much about humanity watching her run that diner single-handedly for years after my *papou* died.

My childhood experience as a Greek American taught me to have a strong work ethic and to treat all the workers with dignity, respect, and appreciation, regardless of their backgrounds. The employees returned that in spades through their hard work and loyalty. The workplace cultures I aspire to achieve today reflect what I learned growing up as a Greek American—environments that inspire love, joy, respect, and a warm welcome for everyone.

Anthony J. Limberakis, MD, Archon Aktouarios, National Commander of the Order of Saint Andrew and Chair of the Ecumenical Patriarch Bartholomew Foundation

My story begins like so many American Dreams, with an immigrant's hope for a better life. In 1915, my grandparents, Andonios and Evangelia, were victims of violent persecution in Turkey during *the Great Catastrophe*. They fled to America, were rejected from Ellis Island, and spent two years in Mexico until they were granted entry into the safe haven of the United States. Their pockets were empty, but their souls possessed something that **transcends all temporal riches—their faith in God and their Hellenic values:** *Philotimia, Philoxenia, and Philanthropia*: love of honor, love of strangers, and love of humankind. These values are the foundation of my heritage; they are the impetus behind every decision, success, and sacrifice. Just as they guided my beloved *pappou* and *yiayia*, they have compelled me to live a life in service of others: to the Holy Mother Church as an archon, to humankind as a physician, and to my family as a husband and father.

Philotimia, or love of honor, is perhaps the most important Hellenic value. Conceived in ancient Greece, it cannot be easily translated into the modern English vernacular. *Philotimia* is a commitment to the good, to always doing the right thing; even though the right thing is often the most difficult to do. It is a way of life. My parents, a priest and *presvytera*, were the personification of *philotimia* and exemplified living a life in service to Jesus Christ and His flock. My devotion to the Holy Mother Church is rooted in *philotimia*, and ultimately is what drove me to help establish the Ecumenical Patriarch Bartholomew Foundation, an initiative to secure the financial freedom of the Holy Mother Church in perpetuity. This was the right thing to do for the Ecumenical Patriarchate, as well as for His All-Holiness Bartholomew, the longest serving Ecumenical Patriarch in the history of Christianity, for whom the foundation is named.

Philoxenia, or love of strangers, is another value intrinsic to Hellenism and instilled in me by my parents. A defining moment of my childhood was when I was in the car with my family and my father saw a disabled man in a wheelchair struggling to push himself across a busy intersection. He pulled over, parked the car, and pushed the man across the street. As seemingly inconsequential as this act of kindness was, it continues to live within me as a powerful reminder to love thy neighbor. *Philoxenia* inspired a love of engaging with all people, from serving as president of my high school class of eight hundred, to serving as a page in the United States Senate, to serving as president of the Duke Medical Alumni Association, to serving my community as a radiologist. This steadfast love enabled me to overcome every challenge that accompanied owning a freestanding radiology practice for over thirty years so that I could serve my patients.

Philanthropia, like *philotimia* and *philoxenia*, is grounded in love—love of humankind. *Philanthropia* is a calling to live a life in service of others. Personally, this calling has profoundly impacted my life. While my full-time profession is a radiologist, my higher calling is to serve Jesus Christ and our Holy Orthodox faith. I have been blessed with the great privilege and honor to serve the Ecumenical Patriarchate through my service as national commander of the Order of Saint Andrew, with the blessings of Archbishop Spyridon, Archbishop Demetrios and now, Archbishop Elpidophoros of America. Fighting for the religious freedom for the Holy Mother Church and all Christians is a ministry of *philanthropia*, an act of love, that I have embraced fully since my investiture as an archon in 1987. Give well and give often, whether it be your time, talent, or treasure; for as Saint Paul advises, "Do not neglect to do good and to share what you have, for such sacrifices are pleasing to God."

The most hallowed family heirlooms Andonios and Evangelia passed down, generation to generation, were faith in Jesus Christ and their Hellenic values of *philotimia, philoxenia,* and *philanthropia.* These values are woven into the fabric of my heart, mind, and soul. They are my DNA. Most importantly, leading a life with the values of our heritage would not be possible without my beloved wife, Maria, also a physician. Maria is my personal source of inspiration and encouragement. We work together to live impactful lives and continue the legacy of love of honor, love of strangers, and love of humankind to our children and grandchildren.

George M. Logothetis, Chairman and CEO of the Libra Group

The Greek gene means having a gene that learned from oppression, from difficulty, from hardship, from having less. From having to create something from nothing. From having to fight, having to be resilient. Today, the survivors of that genetic coding include 20 million Greeks—ten million living in Greece and ten million who live elsewhere. These shared experiences from our ancestors live on through our DNA.

Think about it. Throughout history, Greeks were always fleeing. They were running. Just like the Jews, the Armenians, the Lebanese. Wherever you travel in the world, there are always strong Greek, Jewish, and Armenian communities. They're the product of oppressed people, but they're also the genetic survivors of an oppressed people. This legacy also gives the ability to be friendly with random strangers and to become friends with people all over the world. The source of that is the wandering warrior of the Greeks.

The understanding of the bloodline and history of how much the Greek people suffered during time, especially the past 500 years, only gives you gratitude for what we have today. That also comes with a responsibility. That ancestral gene, that surviving gene, that Hellenistic gene of resilience and resolve that is embedded in all of us as Greeks. This is *philotimo*, the ability to be in the arena fighting and still keep your principles at an even keel. To modulate the animal instincts to be aggressive and be sensible and wise. To know that the happiest people are those who give, not those who take.

The industrious Greek, the thoughtful Greek. The Greek who acts with *philotimo*, who is able to just be kind especially in the face of cruelty. The Greek who is thoughtful of others. The Greek whose philanthropic code is premised on that most ancient coding which is to give without expecting to get.

Before the United States of America was born in 1776, the world was ruled. After the United States of America was created, the world started to be governed—it wasn't governed, it *started* to be governed. And the genesis of the United States Constitution and the freedoms we enjoy today, come from 2,000 years ago from the Greeks. Greece gave light to the world, then many dark years came, then America relit the fuse of brightness. Our genetic legacy is deeply Greek, and also at the heart of the United States. How great do we have it in the United States in 2022 in spite of everything? Just flick through the pages of history and you will understand.

As a Greek American, I am so appreciative. Grateful. Humbled. Indebted. Freedom is written into our DNA, and the empathy and love of freedom for others. This is one of the gifts of our ancestors that we can give to the world.

Maria Loi, Chef, Restauranteur, and Author

I started my life in a small village in Greece as a farm girl. The values that I got from my parents and the local teacher growing up in this environment shaped my life in countless ways.

My parents raised me to understand the value of hard work and the importance of a close-knit family—we five children, of whom I was the youngest, were lucky to have these values woven so deeply into the fabric of our being. To this day I am close to my siblings, and to this day it is hard work that brings me meaning.

Growing up, we were taught to never give up, no matter what—there's always a solution to be found. When I faced a seemingly difficult situation, my parents showed me how to look at it from different perspectives and find an alternative approach. This has given me strength throughout my life, not just as a business woman, or a chef, but as a human being.

They also taught me that though you can be strong, it is important to also be compassionate, sensitive, and kind—they used to tell me, "When you see a child in distress, your heart should melt, and the urge to help them should overwhelm you." It is these words that I hear in my mind, that drive me to dedicate my philanthropic efforts toward helping children.

Perhaps the most important value I hold dear is the uniquely Greek notion of *philotimo*. Though hard to define in English, in essence it means to do good, by doing things with a sense of pride, love, and respect—respect for oneself and for others; for one's family; and for one's people.

The only way to truly understand what *philotimo* means is to be born to it; I'm proud and happy that I was born into a Greek family, whose love, support, and values made me into the person that I am today. To find happiness and meaning is the biggest success in life. *Philotimo* has helped me find it.

Congresswoman Nicole Malliotakis, Member of Congress

My father instilled in me to be proud of my Greek heritage and roots from a very young age. He taught me that the Greeks are strong people that have contributed to society at every level. From democracy to astronomy, medicine to mathematics and philanthropy, Greeks have made significant contributions in nearly every aspect of our lives.

I always knew I was different than the rest of my classmates when I was younger. Being Greek and Cuban and growing up in an Italian American community, it was easy to feel like an outcast, but my father always made me feel proud about my Greek heritage.

As I got older and involved in a church where I met other Greeks, I always sensed a certain bond. You get excited when you meet someone who is not only Greek but then from your island. It's a very Greek feeling. You feel connected; you feel like family.

My father is from Sitia and most people you meet in America are from Chania, Heraklion, or Rethimno. For me, when I meet someone from Sitia, it's a big deal. I think that's what makes the Greek community so special. They are willing to help each other, embrace each other, and support one another regardless of personal politics. You share the values of Greek heritage and that is what matters. Greeks support other Greeks; they want to embrace you and be a part of your success along the way.

One thing that always struck me about the Greek people is their work ethic. My father is one of the hardest-working people I've ever met, and this work ethic and pride in productivity are echoed in every Greek American I have come to meet. When he first came to this country, he had three jobs. Before my father retired, he had a small business and worked a second job as a banquet waiter. I always remember him coming home very late from his second job which greatly impacted me. My father worked very hard; he sacrificed for me, the next generation, so I could do better.

Greek people who have been given the opportunity to achieve the American Dream often do because of this Greek work ethic. Greeks are creative, and they'll always find a way to solve problems with what they have. For this reason, Greeks can be found at all levels of business, politics, and philanthropy. I am proud to be a part of this Greek family, one of hard work ethic and dedication to God, family, and country.

John G. Manos (Manoukarakis), President of Bank Financial; Former President of the PanCretan Association of America

I immigrated here with my mother, father, and baby sister in 1967 and have fond memories of the large extended family and small village that we left behind in Crete. Immigrating to a new land, my parents did not speak English but with the help of my great-aunt Sophie, who was already here, they went hard at work from day one to make this new land their home. One of their main goals was to raise and educate their children, no matter what it took. I saw them struggle from job to job to get the next best opportunity, to move from a small apartment to another and ultimately to buy their first home. As time went on, they made their investments and lived the American Dream.

Much of their passion and persistence, I learned later, had to do with their upbringing. They learned to fight for what they wanted, from their history and from what their parents went through: world wars, the depression, and civil war. My parents sent me back to go visit Crete and our family there for the first time seven years later in 1974. I will never forget that trip. The entire village lined up to greet me, this is little *Yannaki*. Then at the age of 14, not so little anymore. I could not get enough of everyone there or the beauty of the village itself.

That trip is where for the first time, I met my grandfather, Stathi Loukogeorgaki, who would forever change my life with his stories of his trip to America in 1911 and his part in the battle with the Germans at the Battle of Crete in World War II. And ... he spoke a little broken English!

His story of coming over on a ship, through Ellis Island (which I later traced him through) was incredible to me. He was talking to me about cowboys and Indians! Going through Ellis Island, to New York, through Chicago and ultimately further west to Price, Utah, where they told him jobs were plentiful. In going there, he immediately started work in the coal mines. He said, "I could carry the world on my shoulders, but I could not do without seeing the sun!" After working in the mines for six months, he quit and went to work at a large farm as a sheepherder. He was a hard worker and always took care of the elderly farmer and his wife. The farmer took to liking him and in a short time became the supervisor of the staff there. The old farmer approached him one day and told him that he was sick and did not have much longer to live. He promised him that if he took care of his wife and the farm, that he would leave him half of his farm. Not very long after that he passed, and the wife passed a few years later. They had no children or family and thus left the entire farm to him. He worked hard and grew the farm to be one of the biggest in the area, with a good reputation and a good name for himself. He helped many new young immigrants coming from Greece, gave them a bed to sleep in, and a job if they wanted one until they could get on their feet.

He was there for seven years and one day he took his horse and buggy with a worker to go to the general store in town to buy feed and supplies that they needed. When he came out of the store, an Indian who was drunk, was assaulting his worker. My grandfather broke them up and the Indian now came to attack him. He pushed him, once, twice, and the third time he pushed him to the ground. The Indian got up and pulled out his knife to attack him. At this point, my grandfather pulled out a gun and shot him dead! There were many townspeople there at the time and the store owner all witnessed what happened so when the sheriff came, they concluded that it was self-defense and to go home. A few days later, there was a knock on the door very early in the morning. It was the mayor and the sheriff advising him that the Indian he had shot was the chief's son and if he wanted to live and he wanted to help save the town, that he would have to leave! After much thought, he decided to move back home. He sold the farm and all of his belongings, he turned his cash into gold coins, stuffed them in small round cheese balls which he put in his backpack, so they wouldn't rob him on the train, and took the train to New York and the ship back to Crete.

This is the same grandfather that I saw photos of with the British ambassador, hanging in the living room in the village, in Vilandredo, Rethymno, Crete. He was one of the heroes of the Battle of Crete who abducted General Krieper in May of 1941! There are books and a few movies made of this amazing story where they talk about his role in the abduction. Many say that this changed the course of history, since the 10-day delay to take over Greece caused the Germans to go into Russia a week and a half late and ran into a terrible winter storm that handicapped them and caused them to lose the battle and ultimately the downfall of their war!

That summer that I was there, the summer of 1974, was the Turkish occupation of Cyprus, as my uncle was getting ready to leave to go to the army as many of age had gotten the call. I was there on the veranda next to my grandfather. At one point, with all the family around him, he went quiet and then slammed down his *bastouna* and proclaimed, "I should be 15 years younger and I would be the first in line to go fight them!"

These are the true heroes, these are the people that we need to learn from. He did not give up growing up in poverty, he did not give up in Utah, he did not give up with the Germans. From his stories I learned to stand proud, I learned to fight for what I want, for me and for my family. To fight for what is right and just. Don't give up and never stop striving for your dream! Do whatever it takes to succeed. Support and help others—it will come back to you!

George M. Marcus, Founder and Chairman of Marcus & Millichap; Philanthropist

Fifty-seventy percent of young men at the turn of the century—the 1880s, 1890s, and 1900s—left Greece to places like South Africa, Australia, and New Zealand. Basically, they went where labor was needed and labor bosses would pay their way; they would earn money and then pay them back. My father left at the age of 14 and ended up in Argentina. He worked there for a number of years. His brother came to San Francisco, so he decided to come there. He did so illegally. He jumped ship from New Orleans in about 1910/1912. In 1920 there were at least two amnesties for illegals and I bet half of the United States was in amnesty in one way or another.

One-third of immigrants from all countries in Europe went back to their countries because they wanted economic success, but not cultural fusion. So, like all Greek men did, he went back to Evia and had an arranged marriage with my mother. My poor mother spoke no English and was dragged across the country to a little town in California—Potrero Hill. It had every single ethnic group in the entire world.

I was born in Greece. Because when my father was in San Francisco, he worked as a laborer next to Italian immigrants, he spoke Spanish and Italian when he went back to Greece. So on the island of Evia, he was the only Italian-speaking Greek while the Italians occupied it. We kind of survived and everything was fine even though it was horrifying. Something like one-third of Greeks in urban cities in 1942 starved to death. My father was in Evia and his family were cheesemakers, so they had sheep and goats. Greece was a catastrophe after the war ended in 1945, so my father returned to the United States because he was a citizen. He had to start all over again.

And now comes my journey. When we returned to the US, I spoke nothing but Greek. We lived in a neighborhood with lots of different nationalities. I had one differentiation. All my friends could play outside for as long as they wanted, but I had to be home by 5:00 to do my homework.

So my journey started with more discipline than any of my friends, more focus on education. Education was driven into my brain and I basically got the message. During this time there was a lot of military draft, so I decided to join the army which was when my instincts developed. I did a lot of odd jobs. I managed the post theater and had tons and tons of activities. I was going to the University of Maryland night school. I got out early and came back to San Francisco where I went to San Francisco State. I had a part-time job but graduated in two years with a BS in economics. Later on, I got appointed as a trustee of the state university system. I also was appointed to be a University of California regent which is a plum appointment.

When I got out of school, I thought corporate America was my savior. I figured I'd become a CEO of a company, but I had no idea how or why. So I took a job at the Bank of America. I thought that the harder you work, the more you are recognized, but my boss called me in to tell me, "You don't understand. You are working too hard; you are doing too much; slow down." And my entire life caved in. I thought I was over. I did what I thought Horatio Alger did. I read all these books and said, what is wrong with this?

So I left after one year and went into a family business and thought this is better. But guess what—if you aren't a member of the family, you don't get promoted. So I found myself going to work for a company that sold real estate. I had a wonderful manager there. Sometimes you just get lucky with someone who cares for you and is knowledgeable and a terrific person. I became more and more specialized in investments in income-producing property.

I then started my own company. We now have a public company called Marcus & Millichap and a public real estate investment trust called Essex. It is the most successful, or pretty close, for investors, producing over 15 percent a year for 25 years for our investors. No one, not even Warren Buffet, makes those kinds of returns.

We are all paid by the hour. You have got to put the time in. There is no other way. You might get lucky and invent something, but that's really a long shot. Concepts are very interesting, but 80–90 percent of success is execution. You have to have very high standards in your behavior in and out of the office. Desire to be good means you have to put the time in, to study, and do the best job you can do.

Execution. Execution. Execution.

Dennis Mehiel, Former President of Largest Independent Manufacturer of Corrugated Boxes; Chairman of the Friends of Saint Nicholas; Philanthropist

He Isn't Even Greek

My *yiayia* and *papou* emigrated from Smyrna about a century ago. *Papou* had been drafted into the Turkish army where his life expectancy could be measured in weeks, if not days. Very typical story of elevating the family one generation at a time. Like most Hellenes, *Papou* had an entrepreneurial streak and was able to open a grocery store in Massachusetts. But the depression came and he lost his business. The family moved to a five-story tenement in the Washington Heights neighborhood of northern Manhattan where the rent was less than $25 a month. He got a job as a janitor, cleaning offices at night; he went to work each afternoon in a suit and tie. *Yiayia* was a seamstress who took in work from neighbors. We worshipped at St. Spyridon every Sunday.

My father had a very high IQ, graduated from an elite merit-based high school at 16, having skipped two years of grade school and to this day is the smartest person I have ever met. At 15 he had a job at Hansom's Bakery at Audubon Avenue and 175th Street. He earned $12 a week, and each Friday, he was required to come home with his pay envelope unopened and give it to *Papou*, who would give him $2 of the $12—the rest went to help support the family.

A pilot during World War II, and after a brief and unsuccessful period in the fur coat business (Greek entrepreneurial streak), he went back into the army, joining the Counter Intelligence Corps—he became a spy and served all over the world for 30 years. A consistent requirement in the service was to attend training schools from time to time and he was generally the number one student. During one period when he was assigned to school at Fort Holabird in Baltimore, there was another serviceman who was extremely smart and also a top student in the class. As I listened, my father told my mother about him one evening, noting that he was the brightest guy in the class, "and he isn't even Greek."

That ingrained pride in our heritage and belief in our never-ending pursuit of excellence have sustained me throughout my life, and it is to what I attribute whatever success I have enjoyed.

C. Dean Metropoulos, Chairman and CEO of Metropoulos & Co.; Philanthropist

It is with great humility and gratitude that I recognize the sacrifices and hardships faced by my parents who took our family out of our Greek village, and brought us to our beloved America, the land of opportunity, to provide us an education and to nourish and fulfill our visions, dreams, and potential. Their love and ethics were the cornerstones to our values and confidence that enabled us to pursue our successful careers and honor our wonderful families.

I have been blessed in my own life's journey, having lived, worked, and traveled for many years in every continent of the world and having enjoyed my beautiful family and that of my sister's and brother's.

I am also very grateful to my wife, Marianne, who has been the true pillar and guide to our very busy family, and to my sons, Evan and Daren, who have been an integral part of the global success of our acquisition business, Metropoulos & Co. Through 87 international acquisitions, plus seven SPACs, they have helped lead the transformation of many companies with innovation, unique marketing, and unmatched sales execution.

Our family, through the Metropoulos Family Foundation and the Giving Pledge, is very committed to philanthropy and environmental stewardship. We work in partnership with many wonderful organizations to try and make a difference both to important causes and to the lives of the so many, far less fortunate children in the world. Some of these include: The Giving Pledge, Memorial Sloan Kettering (cancer research), The Prince's Trust International program for youth education, and many causes supporting abused animals, and underprivileged, sick children—Hole in the Wall Gang, the Campaign to End Childhood Hunger, Shriners Hospitals for Children, etc., as well as several environmental causes.

My family's commitment to "giving" back is an important motivation and the core to our values that truly bring fulfillment and happiness in our lives.

In summary, for young people pursuing successful lives—get educated and pursue your dreams and commit to a strong work ethic to fulfill them. Build a passionate engagement and commitment to all of your endeavors, business, or family, and to whatever extent possible, be generous and sympathetic to the many less fortunate and to causes confronting humanity—environment, medical research, etc.

A well-balanced life includes embracing family, career fulfillment, and philanthropy.

Ambassador John Negroponte, Vice Chairman of McLarty Associates; Former Director of National Intelligence; Former US Ambassador

My parents were both of Greek descent. My mother, Catherine Coumantaros, was actually born in New York City in 1916, but was brought back to Greece by my grandparents in 1918 or 1919, after the end of WWI. Her entire upbringing and education were in Athens, where she was one of the few Greek women who studied law. She was also a markswoman with both rifle and pistol and competed successfully in Balkan games. I still have a couple of her trophies. Though born in the US, my mother was culturally Greek. My mother's parents were from Sparta, although they lived in Athens for many years, where my grandfather owned, along with his three brothers, the flour mill in Piraeus. He also was at one time a member of the Greek Parliament. My Coumantaros grandparents returned to the States during WWII and my grandfather passed away in New York City in 1948. My father, Dimitri Negroponte, was born in Lausanne, Switzerland, on March 25, 1915, the anniversary of Greek independence. He was brought up in Switzerland until he went off to university in Paris in the early 1930s. My Negroponte grandfather was part of the diaspora generated by the Massacre of Chios in 1822. His family escaped from Chios, first to Trieste and then to the Black Sea area of Russia. In fact, my father's father was born in Taganrog, Russia, which as it turns out is only about a two hour drive east from Mariupol, the scene of very heavy fighting in the current war between Ukraine and Russia. At that time, the family was involved in shipping and the export of grain from that area. But their fortunes turned with the onset of WWI and the Russian revolution and they ended up moving to Switzerland. Because my grandmother had tuberculosis, she ended up spending the final years of her life (she died at age 43) in a sanatorium in Davos, which later was no doubt converted into a tourist hotel. Whenever I attend the World Economic Forum (WEF) meetings in Davos, I cannot help but conjure up images of my grandmother whom I had never known but who my father adored so much and had lost at the age of 18. Because of the Davos connection, my father went to a boarding school in Klosters down the valley for a number of years. As a result, he became a competitive skier and took part in the 1936 Winter Olympics in Garmisch as one of two members of the Greek Ski Team. One can confirm through the internet that he did compete in those Olympics, but one also learns that he did not make a very good showing!

My parents met in Greece in 1936 or 1937 and got married in Paris on September 30, 1938, just at the time of the ignominious Munich Agreement. They knew war was coming and did not want to delay their marriage for the sake of a more formal, family event in Athens, where my mother's parents and siblings resided at the time. They settled in London for a brief period, where my father worked in an uncle's shipping office and I was born in a London hospital on July 21, 1939. WWII broke out on September 3 of the same year and my parents quickly decided to leave England for the United States. We arrived in New York City in the latter part of September 1939 aboard the SS *President Harding*, having passed through a horrific hurricane en route across the Atlantic. We then settled into New York, where I and, eventually, three other brothers grew up in the same apartment on 75th Street in Manhattan until my parents decided to return to London in 1972, when we brothers were already either grown up or at least in college. During his time in New York, my father had a shipping office downtown, which meant often going to "Jimmy's Kitchen" on Battery Place when we visited dad at his office. During WWII itself my mother was very active in the Friends of Greece, a New York-based philanthropy dedicated to assisting Greece at the time of German occupation. As a child I took Greek lessons, and because of the war, I learned patriotic Greek songs. Although I can't find the photos anymore, I recall being dressed as an evzone and participating at a children's event at Hunter College where many different nationalities were represented. But I would say that my Greek heritage was one of several cultural influences on my youth. There was also a strong Francophone influence because of my father's studies in Switzerland and France. And, in fact, I spent my college junior year in France, at least in part because of that influence.

On October 5, 1960, after graduating from Yale, I entered the

United States Department of State as a junior foreign service officer, leading to a career of 44 years in government, including five U.S. ambassadorships, as well as being the deputy national security advisor under President Ronald Reagan and the first director of national intelligence under President George W. Bush. You might say that only in America could someone transition so quickly from what was essentially an almost completely foreign background to a career path leading to the highest levels of the United States government. And it is an extraordinary statement about the United States that this is a fairly frequent occurrence. It is a real testament to the openness of our society to the diverse peoples and cultures of this world. I believe that Hellenism had a subtle but pervasive influence on my life. First, I was exposed early in life to the fact that the world is made up of a multiplicity of cultures and languages. Not all Americans carry with them a sensitivity to how diverse our society and world are. Second, I was impressed by someone like my father, whose family had left Greece in 1822, literally 200 years ago and almost 100 years before he was born, and yet spoke fluent Greek and remained loyal to Greece and what it stood for. Our ties to Greece also helped me better understand the perspective of a smaller country in this world dominated by real or wannabe superpowers. This is not to mention the powerful intellectual influence of Greek writings from ancient times to the present that have had a direct influence on my thinking and view of the world—Thucydides's *The History of the Peloponnesian War*, Plato's *The Laws*, the life of Socrates, or the unbelievable novels of Nikos Kazantzakis. As Harry Truman was once quoted as saying, "There is nothing new in the world, except the history you have not read." That was a very profound reflection and I believe captures the significance of Greek thought through the ages to the life we are experiencing today.

Congressman Chris Pappas, Member of Congress

My family came to America from a small village on a hilltop in Greece for the same reason as millions before them and after: they were in search of a better life in a place of opportunity and promise.

When they arrived in America, life wasn't easy. But through hard work, determination, and the support of their families and the Greek American community, my great-grandfather founded what would become our family restaurant, the Puritan Backroom. One hundred and five years later it is still in our family, and the legacy and values of my great-grandfather live on. It is a story that would be familiar to many Greek immigrants and immigrants from throughout the world.

Growing up working in our restaurant served as a constant reminder that I am the beneficiary of their journey, their struggle, and their hard work. I don't know if my great-grandfather thought that his descendent would one day serve in the halls of Congress when he set foot in America for the first time over a century ago. But that history and that story are with me each day I have the honor to represent my home in Washington and I do my best to honor that legacy.

The United States and Greece have continued to share our commitment to democratic institutions and celebrate the right of free people to chart their own destiny. And as one of six Greek members of Congress, I'm proud to serve on the Hellenic Caucus where we work to strengthen those ties between Greece and the United States and celebrate and promote Greek heritage and culture in the United States.

The inspiration that led America to declare our independence and assert the right to life, liberty, and the pursuit of happiness was found in ancient Greece, and our system of government finds its literal roots in the Greek language—*demos*, meaning "the people," and *kratos*, meaning "power." Power that is of, by, and for the people.

I would not be who I am or where I am today, without my upbringing in a Greek family, which was so focused on serving others, to pursuing a career in public service. I'm proud to continue to work to ensure that the United States pursues policies that help new

Americans build their own American Dream, just like my own family once did when they arrived from Greece.

John A. Payiavlas, Founder and Chairman of AVI Foodsystems; Philanthropist

My father came to this country in 1921 and went back to Greece and married my mother in 1928. They came to the US with very little education and no assistance from family members.

They settled in Warren, Ohio, and raised my two wonderful siblings and me.

What little success that I have achieved in this wonderful country I owe to my mother and father, both of whom earned a "master's degree"/"doctorate" on how to raise and nourish a family!

It is from them that I learned what I consider "life's reward system"—integrity, putting others first, exceeding expectations, excellence.

Jim and Ted Pedas, Founders of Circle Films; Philanthropists

Our parents instilled in us early in our childhood that the most treasured, valuable asset you have is your *onoma* (your reputation)!

It must be protected at all costs and at all times. It will open more hearts and more doors for you in your life's journey than any other asset you may have. Our father said, "So don't ever mess it up!"

Paulette Poulos, Executive Director, The Archbishop Iakovos Leadership 100 Fund, Inc.

My life's journey was guided by my Greek American heritage and my faith as a Greek Orthodox Christian. I joined the staff of the Greek Orthodox Archdiocese in 1965 and planned to stay for just one year because I intended to pursue my education to become a CPA.

I never dreamed that the years would go by so fast and that I would devote my entire professional career to serving the church. I recall my first interview with Archbishop Iakovos of Blessed Memory who told me, "You will never regret your service to the church which will prove to be one of the most meaningful decisions you will ever make in your life." As I now reflect on that day, I realize how correct he was! Thanks to the vision of Archbishop Iakovos, I was afforded the unique opportunity to use my talents to pave the way for other young women to serve the church.

With the blessings of His Eminence, I served in numerous positions at the archdiocese: Department of Laity, associate director of Youth Ministry, director of the League of Greek Orthodox Stewards (LOGOS), administrative assistant to Archbishop Iakovos, and currently as the executive director for The Archbishop Iakovos Leadership 100 Fund, Inc. I also served on the National Commission for Youth, the Governing Board of the National Council of Churches, and helped raise major capital funds for the Archbishop Iakovos Library and Resource Center at Hellenic College/Holy Cross Theological School.

I was privileged to serve under the spiritual leadership of Archbishop Iakovos, Archbishop Spyridon, Archbishop Demetrios, and presently Archbishop Elpidophoros and have received much recognition over the years. The most recent was the honor bestowed upon me by His Eminence Archbishop Elpidophoros as a senator for Orthodoxy and Hellenism.

As I look back upon these past five decades, I have witnessed firsthand the growth of our church in America, the recognition of our church in becoming a major faith in America, and the development and expansion of National Ministries, which have enhanced our faith and helped the faithful to become more involved in the life of the church.

I will always be grateful for the path that I chose to serve the church and the Holy Archdiocese. I can honestly say I received so much more than I was able to give! I was fortunate to be raised by immigrant parents who instilled in us pride in our Greek heritage and our faith. I will always be grateful to them for raising my siblings and me in the church and providing the proper foundation and values for us to follow throughout our lives.

I smile when people tell me that I am a "role model" because I do not view my service in that manner. However, if I have in any way influenced young women to assume positions in the church, then I will consider it a great accomplishment.

Michael Psaros, Co-founder and Co-managing Partner of KPS Capital Partners, LP; Philanthropist

Being a Greek American and an Orthodox Christian has informed every aspect of my life. Like all Greek Americans, I grew up in two worlds, one Anglo and the other Hellenic. From the youngest age, I realized that I am different and take pride in being different. I fully understand that I am not just a hyphenated American. I know exactly where I am from—the island, the village, and even the house. This knowledge provides me with a sense of place and that is powerful. This knowledge grounds me. This knowledge provides me with dignity and pride.

I thank God that I was raised with the values, value system, respect, traditions, and work ethic resident in every Greek American family, along with accompanying obligations and expectations. I carry that value system with me every day.

The combination of our Hellenic heritage and Holy Orthodoxy is the foundation of my success, not only in business, but much more importantly, as a husband, father, son, and brother.

I am exceedingly proud of the success of the Greek American diaspora in the United States. The success achieved by Greek Americans in only one or two generations is truly extraordinary. I am proud that my family is part of this success story. My paternal grandfather was a refugee from the genocide of Asia Minor. When he immigrated to America, he became a barber in a steel town. His scissors paid for eight college degrees. When my maternal grandfather immigrated to America to that same steel town, his pants were torn when he arrived. He had to borrow money to buy a new pair of pants. The retail store he owned paid for five college degrees. My grandparents did not speak English when they immigrated and had no formal education or money, but they did have hope, faith, and love. Their work ethic was second to none. They sacrificed everything for their children and our family's future. I think about their sacrifice every day. It humbles me. As a member of our family's second generation, I know that it is my obligation to sacrifice everything for the third generation, my children and their children. This is the essence of being a Greek American.

I try to live my life with *philotimo,* the most important foundational element of Greek culture. As a Greek American there is nothing more important to me than my name and reputation, which in turn reflects how I conduct myself personally and professionally every day. A Greek cannot live his life without *philotimo* and neither can I.

Central to living life with *philotimo* is practicing philanthropy. My family is blessed. We try to follow the exhortations of St. John Chrysostom and the example of my two grandmothers regarding the moral obligation to help others. The practice of philanthropy and philanthropic leadership are unbelievably important to me and my family, and I pray my children continue our family's good works for generations to come.

I am blessed to be part a culture that has been a beacon to the world for over two millennia and a faith that is God's gift to the world.

Jeannie Ranglas, President of Metropolis of San Francisco Philoptochos

When I think about my life, starting as a young Greek American girl in Chicago, going to church with my *yiayia*, I have so many fond memories of how both my faith and culture contributed to who I am today.

Being Greek Orthodox is a privilege and one that I have treasured throughout my life. The church has provided me with a place to learn, to grow and develop spiritually, to serve others, to show love and compassion, and to give back to the Lord from the blessings He has given to me and my family.

I cannot separate my faith from my heritage because they are intricately intertwined. When I think about joining Philoptochos at the young age of 22, newly married, and trying to find a place where I could make a difference, my heart fills with gratitude at the opportunities that were granted to me through my involvement with Philoptochos and my parish, where I continue to serve after 45 years.

I remember with great pride and joy watching my children grow up in the church, seeing them perform at the Folk Dance and Choral Festival, helping with the beautiful Greek costumes, and realizing that the heritage I cherished as a child is now being passed down to my children.

And now, I am a *yiayia*. I have seen both my children thrive in various church activities. My daughter, who attended Philoptochos meetings as a toddler, now has a toddler of her own, and she is learning about serving and giving—you're never too young or too old to learn.

I am proud of my heritage because it has provided me with a wide array of experiences that have shaped my life. The language, the cooking, the dancing, the customs and traditions are all vivid reminders of our ancestors who came from Greece to start a new life in this country so they could provide for their families. I have also personally witnessed this in my husband, Gerry, who was born in Greece and built a successful business through hard work, honesty, and integrity. These are hallmark characteristics of being a Hellene, and I am proud that my family still holds fast to these as guiding principles in our lives.

Having served now for more than a decade as the Metropolis of San Francisco Philoptochos president, I have also found that the hospitality we demonstrate to those in need has provided people with a glimpse into how we, as Greek Orthodox Christians, have woven together the strong characteristic of *philoxenia* and blended it with *philotimo* so that we are living examples of Christ's Gospel.

Congressman John Sarbanes, Member of Congress

I reach for my Greek heritage often. The story of my own family has immense power—what it meant for my ancestors to leave Greece and come to this country, anxious yet filled with confidence and optimism about what America could offer. In 1909, still a teenager, my grandfather said goodbye to his tiny village in southern Greece to make the trip through Ellis Island and a new life in America. My grandmother came a few years later from the same part of Greece and together they raised a family that embodied the American Dream. Reflecting on this inspiring journey makes me even more determined that the opportunities afforded to my family be equally available to all Americans.

As Greeks, we put tremendous emphasis on the idea of excellence, of being worthy. We recognize that success in life comes from hard work, playing by the rules and a deep commitment to family and community. Those values—often captured in the word *philotimo*—have animated my personal and professional life. They encouraged my civic engagement at an early age and ultimately drove my interest in public office and service to my constituents.

Like all Greeks, I am immensely proud of the well-founded claim that our ancient ancestors invented democracy. With that honor, however, comes the responsibility to do all we can to preserve democracy in the modern age. My efforts in Congress over a period of 15 years to strengthen American democracy with broad and transformative policy prescriptions is traceable directly to that sense of responsibility.

Drawing on the example of our own traditions to give back to the broader society represents Hellenism in the public service. It is the greatest tribute we can pay to our Greek heritage and to the melting pot that is America. It is how and why we will always aspire *st'anotera*—to greater heights!

Dean A. Spanos, Controlling Owner and Chairman of the Board of the Los Angeles Chargers; President of the A.G. Spanos Companies; Philanthropist

My Greek heritage is as much a part of me as my fingerprint. My parents were both extremely proud of their Greek heritage and my fondest family memories are centered around celebrating our cherished holidays and traditions. Faith, family, and Greek school were how I was raised. My mom and dad embraced the ideals of Hellenism and it naturally filtered down through the entire family ... and it resonated with me. I watched and learned as my father lived a life helping others. I watched him grow an incredibly successful construction company—and live the American Dream—all while holding true to his Greek Orthodox faith and heritage. It made an impression ... and honestly, it impacts me to this day.

No matter where I go—I remember who I am and where my family comes from. My dad's success, and mine, is part of a deep understanding that being an American of Greek descent means having the best of two worlds.

The Honorable Mariyana T. Spyropoulos, Commissioner, Metropolitan Water Reclamation District of Greater Chicago

My DNA is from a nationality that celebrates its culture, history and religion. We are hard-working, entrepreneurial and family oriented.

Our family was ever present and supportive. I love that our elders are taken care of and treated with the dignity and respect that they deserve. Inter-generational gatherings are the norm and provide the support we need in our everyday life.

My family is proud of our heritage and I have carried that sense of pride with me. My parents are immigrants to the United States seeking a better life. I am influenced by their sense of purpose yet pride in their heritage. Hard work and giving back are the pillars of my life which I inherited from my parents and all of their sacrifice.

My Greek heritage has been the foundation of my life.

James Stavridis, Retired US Navy Admiral and Supreme Allied Commander of NATO; Chairman of the Board of the Rockefeller Foundation; and Best-selling Author

My grandparents were Anatolian Greeks who came out of a horrific setting as refugees, fleeing the burning of Smyrna. My grandmother as a teenager was rescued by Greek fishermen as the city burned behind her. What do I take away from that? What are the qualities that personify the Greek experience?

Top of my list is that I have always found Greek Americans to be optimistic … to be believers that things can get better no matter how dark the moment. We can sometimes see that glass half empty, but at the end of the day, there is a streak of optimism that runs through this community. It has served us well over the centuries, and my family's survival reflects that.

Second thing is ambition. I think a healthy dose of ambition is that catalyst, the shot of espresso, that drives you every day. It is a good thing to be ambitious and to achieve. Ambition is a spur that drives us along in this community. And tied to that is a respect for education in bettering each of us and allowing us to fulfill our ambitions.

Third—patriotism figures in the Greek American community. We are patriots. *Patrioti* is a word I use often. There are many ways to serve this country, and Greek Americans are represented in all of them: military, diplomats, Peace Corps, intelligence community, medical, teachers, on and on. To all the Greeks who serve, I say: thank you for your service!

Athan Stephanopoulos, President of NowThis

The story of my family's Greek American experience has always been inextricably linked to that of the church. My *papou* (on my father's side) brought his young family to the United States as a priest to serve the growing Greek immigrant community working in the mines and railways of the Mountain West, finding himself transplanted from a small village in northwest Peloponnese to the foothills of Great Falls, Montana. His two sons, my uncle and my father, both grew up to become priests as well. And it was at Zoodohos Peghe Church in the Bronx where my father met my mother, where she was serving as the organist.

Aside from the influence the church played in my own family's life, it's undeniable the critical role the church has played in keeping our wider Greek heritage—the customs and traditions of our culture—intact. This is true not only here in America but for the Greek diaspora around the world. The church served not only as a place of worship, but as a gathering point for our Greek communities to come together and share in each other's lives during moments of joy and sorrow. It was this communal bond that made you realize you were part of a much larger family and supportive community.

I'm reminded of this type of support from my own personal experiences. For example, when I started my company many years ago, the vast majority of my initial investors were Greeks from across the country. I realize now, years later, that they weren't simply investing in an idea or business opportunity in which they had little understanding, but rather they were also investing in me personally. I will never forget this.

At the core, this is the essence of the Greek spirit and the true meaning of *philotimo*—it's the expression of authentic and unconditional goodness without expecting anything in return. So, what does it mean to be Greek? For me, it's about PRIDE. Pride in our history. Pride in our culture. Pride in our faith. Pride in our self. Pride in our family. And of course, pride in our community.

George Stephanopoulos, Anchor of ABC's *Good Morning America* and *This Week with George Stephanopoulos*

From the very beginning even before I had a job, I knew that I had a family and a broader community rooting for me to catch me if I fell or there to boost me when I needed help. It is such an advantage in this increasingly fractured world to know that you can count on not only your nuclear family but also the broader community.

My dad was born in Greece and his dad was a priest who was assigned to come to the US. My mother was born here and her father had a shoe repair shop that is still, 80 years later, being run by my uncle.

I always felt that I was in that generation grappling to live in both worlds … as I was growing up, our community was the Greek American community built around the church.

Even when I travelled all over the world and went to Greek churches, whether in Greece, Africa, Italy, or elsewhere, it felt familiar with me and a part of my home. It is a great source of comfort.

We knew our parents came here for opportunities and that we were expected to make the best of it. Having that ideal held out both by my parents and the broader Greek community was a great motivator.

Our faith lays out our principles of how you should treat each other, because we are all made in the image of God. Those basic teachings can be interpreted in very different ways. But the basic core values I take from it inform the way I think about everything.

As well, I was raised with the concept of *philotimo*—a perfect word embodying the "Golden Rule" but taking it to an even higher level—to treat others as you would want to be treated, to reach beyond what you expect for yourself and do even better.

Congresswoman Dina Titus, Member of Congress

In 1911, my grandfather came to this country through Ellis Island from Greece. Arthur Costandinos Cathones, for whom I am named, started with little and eventually owned a restaurant in a small town in southern Georgia. Like so many who came before him, he believed in the promise of America, but he never forgot his Greek roots.

The small town I grew up in had no Greek church or school and we would take 100-mile road trips to Jacksonville, Florida, just to get olives and Feta cheese. Yet, even at a young age, my grandfather made sure that my sister and I knew that being Greek is about more than what you eat. He instilled in us the importance of *philotimo*: helping others, giving back to the community, and getting the most out of life.

When I reflect on my heritage and my family, I try to do my best each day to honor their legacy through action. That means following these principles not only in my private life, but also in my public service. So perhaps you will not be surprised to learn that in Congress, I've joined the congressional Hellenic Caucus and fought hard to strengthen the relationship between the US and Greece, opposed the conversion of Hagia Sophia from a museum to a mosque, and worked with my colleagues to bolster security in the Eastern Mediterranean.

Yet, the lessons I learned from my family go far beyond any specific policy positions. Their legacy is why I am always mindful that a public office is a public trust. I believe strongly that serving in any elected capacity is fundamentally about putting others ahead of yourself. Of course, in keeping with the indominable Greek spirit, I try to remind my colleagues and staff to celebrate their accomplishments with a little fun, good food, and dancing.

Fortunately, the halls of Congress are far from the only place where Greek ethos is influencing American life. From church pews to basketball courts and movie studios, our Greek heritage is proudly on display for all to see and experience. I am honored to be considered among this company of Greek American leaders.

Now more than ever, the United States must be a steadfast ally to our longtime partners who share our democratic values. I'll continue to use my voice and my vote to strengthen the bonds between the US and Greece—and I'll do so with my grandfather in mind.

Angelo K. Tsakopoulos, Founder of AKT Development; Philanthropist

I was fourteen years old when I left Rizes to come to America. My mother was actually the one who agreed first and then she convinced my father. I can still hear her voice as she pled my case, "Let the boy go!" By then, my dad was probably tired of hearing me ask again and again to go live in America with my uncles, one of whom was in Chicago and the other in California. When another family from our village was planning to make the trip, my father made arrangements for me to go too.

There is a lot I can still remember about my first months in America. I remember sailing into the port in New York City and seeing skyscrapers that made me feel like I'd landed on the moon. I remember my cousins in Chicago, four giggling girls, making fun of me for not knowing how to properly use a fork and knife. I remember a long train ride to California, past never-ending golden fields of waving grain. I wrote to my father that for hours, you could not see a single stone—unlike in Greece, where we plucked stones out of the soil before we could plant anything. And of course, I remember Lodi.

My uncle Angelo had fought in the First World War in France, along with the allies, and moved to California to pursue his own dream as a farmer. Settling in Lodi, a very small town in the Central Valley, he was living in a fixed-up garage. I'd asked to stay in Chicago with my charming cousins, to live with them in their warm and loving household. But Uncle Angelo had signed the paperwork which gave me status as a refugee, or "displaced person," and he wanted me there to help him with his farming work. Although I was just learning my first words of English, I started school and at the end of each day and on weekends, I worked in the fields along with my uncle and mostly other immigrants, as a farmworker.

People often think that my early years in America must have been very hard. But to tell the truth, I felt I had landed in paradise. My teachers and neighbors were incredibly generous and welcoming to me, and I was able to make enough money to send some home to my family. The harder I worked, the more money I could make. The friendlier I was, the friendlier people were back to me—especially the Fitzer family.

Mom and Pop Fitzer were incredible people. I went to high school with their son, Tim, and little by little, found myself spending time at their house. One day, I came by to check in and Mom asked why she hadn't seen me in a while. By then, I was a senior in high school and had rented a room at the Tokay Hotel. I explained that this way, I could be closer to school and not have to worry about coming home late to disturb my uncle, who woke up hours before dawn. I thought it was a great arrangement but Mom Fitzer did not. "That's skid row! That is no place for a young man of your age!" To make a long story short, Mom and Pop convinced me to stay overnight in Tim's room, and I never left.

It was Pop Fitzer who first raised the possibility of my going to college. I saw limitless opportunity all around me—to work and earn money for myself and my family back home. Graduating high school meant that I could work full time, and I had quite a few plans. But Pop sat me down to go over my report card—something I usually just signed and returned to school myself. He noted that while my English grades weren't great, that's probably because it was my second language. But my grades in math and history were good, and I should continue with my education. At first, I was hesitant. Not just because I was eager to get to work, but because no one had ever before suggested that college was for me. Pop told me that going to college was like climbing a mountain. Along the way, I would meet philosophers, kings, generals, and presidents. I would learn about their lives, the decisions they made, and the consequences of their leadership. When I got to the top of the mountain, he explained, I will see far and wide past Lodi, past Stockton, past Sacramento, and beyond.

I ended up at Sacramento State University, and in many ways, the trajectory of my life was set during my years there. I studied business but also read the Great Books—including Aristotle, whose philosophy I have endeavored since then to make my own. To support myself, I got a job as a waiter at a restaurant popular with the major Sacramento politicos—who were generous with both tips and their advice. Since school only cost $63 per semester including books, there was plenty of money to continue sending home to Rizes.

I fell in love with Sacramento, a beautiful city where over many decades now I have raised my family with my wife, Sofia, and built my business—building master-planned housing developments, and farming. A few years ago, my local newspaper, the *Sacramento Bee*, said that I had changed the face of our town more than anyone since John Sutter, who had discovered gold in 1849 and sparked the gold rush. I'm not sure if that's true or not! But I have had a wonderful career, and along the way, I always took every opportunity to be part of my community.

Ancient Athenians, when they reached the age of citizenship, took an oath to leave their city better than they found it. In my case, I was able to work with leaders and friends from other ethnic groups to help their communities too. I was able to help our first Latino mayor, Joe Serna, establish the La Familia Center to support low-income Hispanic families. Our first Asian congressman, Bob Matsui, and I worked together to build the Asian senior center, and later, the Asian sports center. Our first black mayor, Kevin Johnson, established St. Hope Academy, supporting mostly underserved African American youth, and Sofia and I were able to help him too. Along the way Sofia, our kids, and I were able to donate land for three Greek Orthodox churches, three Mercy Hospitals, as well as a new private university.

My civic involvement has been even more important to me when it's come to our vibrant, national Greek American community. Along with my friends on both sides of the Atlantic: Peter Pappas, Jim Regas, Captain Vasilis Constantakopoulos, Father Alex Karloutsos, John Sitilides, Andy Manatos, George Marcus, and so many others, we worked to improve bilateral relations between Greece and the United States. During the Clinton years, our group helped advise the White House on how to de-escalate tensions during the Imia crises—when Greece and Turkey found themselves on the brink of war.

Greek culture, history, and philosophy are also important to me, and Sofia and I, along with our children, have endowed chairs in Hellenism at Georgetown, Stanford, Columbia, UC Davis, and San

Francisco State University. At my alma mater, Sacramento State, our family established a scholarship program for farmworker children and donated a library of 80,000 volumes of Greek works, curated by Dr. Spiros Vryonis.

I have been very lucky in my life. Sofia and my friends in the Greek community in Sacramento, along with our friends from Leadership 100, Elios, and the National Hellenic Society, have all lived some version of our shared story. Given the opportunity to work hard and give back however possible allowed us to build lives of purpose and joy. Just as Aristotle promises. And when we share a glass of wine, along with *yiasas* and *yiamas,* we say "GBA"! God Bless America! What an incredible country this is, to offer so much to my family, to my fellow Greek Americans and to our fellow immigrants from all corners of the world.

George Tsunis

My heritage is incredibly important to me. In my earliest years, we spoke Greek in the house, exclusively Greek. In kindergarten, I couldn't speak a word of English, so it sort of dominated my early years. My parents both spoke about the small village in Greece, Platanos, Nafpaktias, that they grew up in. They would recount that they grew up in homes that had no running water, no electricity, and an outhouse. There weren't even roads going to the village, there were just pathways. But they would say, "We were poor, but there were times we didn't know it because we were so rich in love and family."

Two of the most important lessons my parents taught me from a very young age were the concept of family being most important and the concept of love. They followed Emma Lazarus' calling and came to the United States. My mom was a seamstress, my dad was a waiter. He later became a very successful restaurant owner. Through their actions, they taught me the importance of hard work. It was absolutely essential. My father was a Depression baby, they lived through World War II, they lived through the civil war in Greece in the late '40s. They were both acutely aware that life was very cruel, starvation was very real, and being out on the street was very real. They lived with that fear when immigrating to this country. Not knowing anyone, scarcely any money in their pockets, they worked really hard. But they worked really hard for their family because they wanted their family to have more opportunities than they had.

Then there was education. Anastasia, Vicki, and I, the three of us all got advanced degrees because education was important. My parents said something very similar to what Senator Paul Sarbanes said about education when he said, "You're going to be educated. I don't care if you're a dishwasher, you're going to be an educated dishwasher." They thought that education and hard work were the keys to success in achieving the American Dream, having a sense of fulfillment, and the actualization of taking care of one's family.

Throughout all of this, there was a greater sense of honor—that you're responsible for things other than your own pecuniary interests or your own family. That we have greater responsibilities. In Hebrew, I like to quote tikkun olam, which is to repair the world one person, one situation, at a time. To care about things other than what our immediate needs are. We Greeks embrace the concept of *philotimo*, where we have a love of honor. There is a reason that Greece has been on the right side of history, always. There is a reason that the Greeks acted to protect their Jewish community during World War II when others did not. And there is a reason that this small community in the United States has achieved such overwhelming success against all odds. We are honor bound to work hard and establish a meritocracy. That's something we pass on to our children, something we identify with. That ethos also requires us to give back. Whether it's to maintain the church or it's to help someone in need or whether it's to teach our children about their roots back in Greece. In this country we are very proud to be Americans but we're also very proud of our Greek heritage.

Argyris (R.J.) Vassiliou, President of Acme Pallet Co. and Di-Cor Industries; Immediate Past Chairman of The Archbishop Iakovos Leadership 100 Fund, Inc.

Pride in my Hellenic heritage was instinctive, having been christened with my *papou*'s name and raised in a two-family home with my Kastorian grandparents. Attendance at Saint Demetrios School in Astoria from kindergarten through eighth grade instilled a devotion to our Greek Orthodox faith and developed my ability to read, write, and speak the Greek language. While initially difficult for a child with a non-Greek mother, this early study of the language, religion, and history of my father's native country, set the foundation for a lifetime love of learning.

The ancient Greek ideal of a sound mind and sound body resonated throughout my life. Involvement with the community began early with St. Demetrios GOYA, Long Island City Sons of Pericles, Hellenic clubs at Stuyvesant High School and Princeton University and it progressed to engagement with parish councils, the Saint Michael's Home for the Aged, to current Anatolia College trusteeship and the chairmanship of the Archbishop Iakovos Leadership 100 endowment, as well as Advisory Council membership at both the Princeton University Art Museum and the Tang Museum at Skidmore College.

While I will always maintain tremendous pride in being American, given all our unrivaled country has offered my family and the entire world, appreciation and love for all things Greek has shaped my being. From the foundations of democracy to the remarkable accomplishments of the most famous Macedonian Greek, Alexander the Great, to General Metaxas' celebrated response of October 28, 1940, through Greece's victory over the communists after the end of World War II, there is much for this Astoria-born son of immigrants to acknowledge and appreciate.

God Bless America and *Zhto H Ellas*!!!

Emmanuel E. Velivasakis, PE, FASCE, Structural Engineer; Former President of the Pancretan Association of America

The Privilege and Responsibility for Being Greek and Especially Cretan

It is truly a privilege to come from the unique place of beauty like Greece, which the gods placed in crystal clear blue waters, between three continents, and to be the crossroads of civilizations from the depths of the centuries. Crete in particular, the place of my birth, is a precious and idiosyncratic part of Greece, a unique place, where you discover the codes and the cultural values that it carries from the depths of the centuries. A place bathed in sunlight, with kind-hearted and proud people, who through their history have generously tasted both glory and death. It is the aroma and taste of *tsikoudia*, the sound of the lyre, the *leventia* of the Cretan, and the pride of Crete.

Crete is the source that quenches our thirst with the "water" of its culture, with the *tsikoudia* of its humanity, it is the mother who gives us measure and time to synchronize our way of life in the countries we live in. From Crete we draw our strength, our musical notes, our thoughts, and our patience. Our Crete, as we know it, as we remember it, has become our experience. An experience that we must always keep relevant to our lives and transmit to our children and grandchildren intact and whole. And this precious Crete, the older we get, the older it grows and reaps within us, to all of us who live far from it. Maybe because we now understand that there is no better place, and no matter how hard we look for it, we will never find it.

Carrying this heavy tradition, it is our obligation to promote the place of our birth, its culture, its history, and the Greek "spirit" in general. But it takes struggle to preserve this treasure! A great struggle is needed to preserve the Greek spirit. It is indeed a great responsibility to be Greek and especially Cretan. Especially in these challenging times we live in, when whole economic systems and societies are in danger of collapsing and an enduring pandemic taking a heavy toll on all of us, we have an obligation to keep the

Greek spirit alive, by preserving it and living by its rules, our Greek identity and the promotion of the values of our race. An even greater responsibility now that humanity and society seem to have taken the wrong turn. Are we ready to accept this extraordinary challenge? I for one believe so, and I want to believe that you too, my dear friends, agree with me on this. The alternatives are not very appealing indeed!

It has been a great honor for me, but also a great challenge to be of Cretan and Greek descent, and to have served as president of the Pancretan Association of America and the World Council of Cretans. Through that role, I had the unique opportunity to have represented Crete and Cretans around the world. As long as I am alive, I will continue to strive toward the great endeavor of keeping our cultural identity vibrant and relevant in our lives and to hope to be worthy of its honor.

The Road Ahead: Will They Take the Torch?

Mike A. Manatos—President of Manatos and Manatos; Executive Director, Washington Oxi Day Foundation

Greek Americans of my generation have benefited enormously from the wisdom, guidance, and hard work of those before us—the immigrants, first and second generations of our proud community. And, in the process, they have helped us fully appreciate the "magic" of Hellenism and Orthodoxy.

Now it is time for us to do the same for our children and grandchildren. As simple as this sounds, it is not. In fact, it is an enormous challenge that weighs heavily on me.

While the raw numbers of Greek Americans have certainly grown over the past 100 years, there has been a sharp decline in the number of Greek Americans who donate their time, talent, and treasure to the promotion and preservation of Hellenism and Orthodoxy nationally. While most of the over 500 Greek Orthodox churches across the country have dedicated, vibrant congregations that serve their local community, the national leadership has changed dramatically. There were thousands in my *papou*'s generation. There are hundreds in my father's generation, though we are losing many by the day. Sadly, there are less than 100 in my generation ... and half that in the next.

I have been blessed to have had a front row seat over the past 50 years to this national effort. As a young man, I watched my *papou*—the first Greek American to work in the White House—and my father—who, among other things, was at the heart of the efforts in the US Congress to impose the US arms embargo on Turkey after its invasion and occupation of Cyprus.

I spent every day of my over 30-year professional career working at my father's side and with other giants in our Greek American community who have been at the forefront of preserving and promoting Hellenism and Orthodoxy. I have learned so much from them and now serve alongside many of them on the boards of several of the top national Greek American organizations.

So, I am intimately familiar with what has been done so far. Yet how I do the same for future generations is very unclear, primarily, because of the complexity of my audience—the future generations.

While our family is known for its over 85 years and three generations of promoting Hellenism and Orthodoxy with US policymakers, the fact is that my children are fourth generation and one-quarter Greek. So the question I often contemplate and what my generation needs to answer is: what does Hellenism and Orthodoxy mean to a fourth generation, 1/4th Greek American? Or, more importantly, how do we make the magic of Hellenism and Orthodoxy relevant to my children and their generation?

I have another unique perspective in this effort. I am the proud son of a Greek Orthodox convert, as well as the proud husband of a Greek Orthodox convert. So, I have also seen firsthand those not born into our community, but who chose to become members, and the love they too have for our community, culture, and faith.

So, in summary, this is our enormous challenge of my generation: there are far fewer of us carrying the torch in the national organizations (and fewer such organizations), and those to whom we are passing it are very different from those who lit it.

While the challenges are many, I do have hope. I have had the opportunity to meet hundreds of young Greek Americans across the country through several impactful programs with which I'm intimately involved through the National Hellenic Society, Leadership 100, the Washington Oxi Day Foundation, the National Hellenic Students Association, Project Mexico and more. And while these students/young professionals are nothing like my *papou* and *yiayia*,

I see deep inside each of them something that is the same. It is what I like to call "the pilot light of Hellenism and Orthodoxy." And *this* is the target. It is the duty of my generation to not only see that pilot light in each but, more importantly, find ways to ignite it. For if we can find aspects of Hellenism and Orthodoxy that excite today's fourth generation, 1/4th Greek American or Greek Orthodox convert, their flame for Hellenism and Orthodoxy can burn just as bright as those who brought the flame to this country.

BIOGRAPHIES

Art Agnos

Art Agnos began his career in San Francisco where he served 11 years as a California state assemblyman followed by four years as mayor of San Francisco, and eight years as a presidential appointee in the Department of Housing and Urban Development.

Agnos was a strong advocate for immigrants and minorities, the homeless, gays and lesbians, health care, affordable housing, and people with AIDS. In 1989, he received national attention for his leadership as mayor after the "Loma Prieta" earthquake. He has been invited to provide seminars on disaster response and governance in South Africa, Angola, Sierra Leone, Palestine, Turkey, Russia, Korea, and China.

Some unique highlights in a very fulfilling life include surviving being shot while volunteering in a public housing project, hosting Soviet Union President Mikhail Gorbachev during his first visit to the US, and befriending Mother Teresa who came to his house unannounced one Sunday evening.

Art and his wife, Sherry, live in San Francisco and have two sons working in the field of sustainability and communications.

Maria Allwin

Maria Allwin worked at Morgan Stanley early in her career before becoming active in the nonprofit arena. Together with her late husband, James M. Allwin, she formed Aetos Capital LLC and the Allwin Family Foundation.

She has served on the parents' board of various institutions, including, among others, the Committee for Education and Technology at the Museum of Modern Art and Communities in Schools. She serves on the Executive Board of Leadership 100, The Ecumenical Patriarch Bartholomew Fund, and the Friends of Saint Nicholas.

Allwin is employed at Trevor Day School, an independent nursery – 12th grade independent school in New York City as assistant to the head of school. Surrounded by brilliant colleagues and students, she is in a position to give back every day to the Trevor community.

Maria Allwin's words to live by are from St Paul: "Keep Alert. Stand firm in your faith. Be courageous. Be strong. Let all that you do be done in love."

John Angelos

For over two decades, John Angelos has led business operations for the Baltimore Orioles, currently as chairman and CEO and MLB Control Person, while also serving as president of the Mid-Atlantic Sports Network (MASN), one of the leading US regional sports media properties reaching millions of television households across seven states.

Recognized as Marylander of the Year Honorable Mention by the *Baltimore Sun*, Angelos has been hailed by industry-bible *Sports Business Journal* as a "power player" and a "top-ten decision maker" on Major League Baseball media and digital issues. He won praise for his "reinvention of the Spring Training business model" in creating taxpayer-conscious, public-private sports tourism development partnerships.

As a longtime thought leader and champion for diversity and civil rights, Angelos' philanthropic focus has been to pioneer the use of sports and media platforms to create community benefit and change. He has created programs fusing sports, diplomacy, and culture through partnerships he developed around women and girls' empowerment, inner city mentoring and job programs, United Nations environmental defense, and the Orioles' Cuba-United States people-to-people sports diplomacy initiatives.

Peter Baker

Peter Baker is the chief White House correspondent for the *New York Times* and a political analyst for MSNBC. He has covered five presidents and currently writes about President Joseph R. Biden Jr. and his administration. He previously covered Presidents Donald J. Trump and Barack Obama for the *Times*, which he joined in 2008, and Presidents Bill Clinton and George W. Bush for the *Washington Post*, where he worked for 20 years. While at the *Post*, he also served as Moscow co-bureau chief, chronicling the rise of Vladimir Putin and covered the opening months of the wars in Afghanistan and Iraq. He is the author or co-author of seven books, including the *New York Times* bestseller, *The Man Who Ran Washington: The Life and Times of James A. Baker III*, with his wife, Susan Glasser, of the *New Yorker,* and named one of the books of the year by the *New York Times Book Review*, the *Washington Post, Financial Times, Fortune* magazine, and *Bloomberg News*. He and Glasser live in Washington with their son and released their latest book *The Divider:Trump in the White House, 2017-2021*, in September 2022.

Drake G. Behrakis

Drake Behrakis is president of Marwick Associates, a real estate investment and development company. Marwick is part of a family-owned investment company. He is also active in the Behrakis Foundation, the family's philanthropic vehicle. Prior to establishing Marwick, Behrakis was with Muro Pharmaceutical and the Gillette Company. He has a bachelor's degree from Boston College and an MBA from Northeastern University.

He serves as chairman of the Board of Trustees of the National Hellenic Society and is on the Board of Directors for The Hellenic Initiative, Boston College, the American College of Greece, Hellenic College/Holy Cross, Delphi Economic Forum, and Leadership 100. He is also on the Board of Overseers at Brigham & Women's Hospital and invested into the Order of Saint Andrew.

In 2015 he received the Boston College Distinguished Volunteer

Award. Previous commitments include member of the Massachusetts Economic Assistance Coordinating Council; Perkins School for the Blind: Sudbury Youth Basketball; the Lowell Plan; Saints Memorial Medical Center; and Fordham University.

Behrakis resides with his wife, three children, and dog, Lola.

Lily Haseotes Bentas

Lily Haseotes Bentas was born in Cumberland, Rhode Island, one of eight children of Vasilios S. and Aphrodite B. Haseotes, both of whom immigrated from Greece in the early 1900s. She spent her entire working career in a company started by her parents. That company, Cumberland Farms, grew from a family farm to one of the largest privately held convenience store/gasoline companies in the US. She held various positions in the company, eventually becoming the CEO and chairperson in 1989. She and her husband, Efthemios, are longtime members of Leadership 100, and support various Greek organizations and educational institutions. In addition, they have supported various medical organizations including Massachusetts Eye and Ear Infirmary and Massachusetts General Hospital where they recently established an endowed fund for cancer research.

Congressman Gus M. Bilirakis

Congressman Gus M. Bilirakis represents Florida's 12th Congressional District in the US House of Representatives. He was first elected to Congress in 2006 and serves on the Energy and Commerce Committee. With 38 bills he authored signed into law since 2015, Congressman Bilirakis was recently designated as the "Most Effective Republican Lawmaker in the State of Florida" by the Center for Effective Lawmaking at Vanderbilt University. He also serves as co-chair of the congressional Caucus on Hellenic Issues.

Bilirakis is the grandson of Greek immigrants and the son of the former member of Congress Mike Bilirakis. His grandfather owned a local bakery where Bilirakis worked from a young age. He graduated from the University of Florida and received his JD degree from the Stetson University College of Law.

The Honorable B. Theodore Bozonelis

B. Theodore Bozonelis is national vice commander and executive committee member of the Order of Saint Andrew the Apostle, Archons of the Ecumenical Patriarchate. He also serves as the secretary officer and executive committee member of the Archdiocesan Council of the Greek Orthodox Archdiocese of America.

He was nominated by the governor of New Jersey and confirmed by the State Senate as a judge of the Superior Court of New Jersey in 1990. In 2003, he was appointed as the assignment (chief) judge for Northern New Jersey Counties, where he oversaw the administration of the state courts and 56 municipal courts therein. In that capacity, Judge Bozonelis served as a chairman and member of the State Judicial Council, which supervises the overall state judiciary. New Jersey Governor Chris Christie appointed him to his State Judicial Advisory Panel, evaluating all state judicial candidates.

Bozonelis received his bachelor's degree from Rutgers University and his JD cum laude from George Washington University.

He and his wife, Helen, an editor and author, have two adult children, Justin and Lia.

Sylvia Mathews Burwell

Sylvia Mathews Burwell is the 15th president of American University in Washington, DC. She previously served as the secretary for the US Dept. of Health and Human Services under President Barack Obama. Prior to that, she was director of the White House Office of Management and Budget (OMB). From 2012 until her appointment at OMB, Sylvia served as president of the Walmart Foundation. She is former president of the Global Development Program at the Bill & Melinda Gates Foundation, where she worked for 11 years and was also the first chief operating officer. During the Clinton Administration, she served as deputy director of OMB, deputy chief of staff to the president, chief of staff to the secretary of the treasury, and staff director of the National Economic Council. Burwell is on the boards of the Council on Foreign Relations, GuideWell, and the Kimberly-Clark Corporation. She received an AB from Harvard University and a BA from Oxford, where she was a Rhodes Scholar. Burwell hails from Hinton, West Virginia. She and her husband, Stephen, live in Washington, DC, with their two children, Helene and Matthew.

John P. Calamos Sr.

John Calamos is chairman and global chief investment officer of Calamos Investments, the firm he founded in 1977. A pioneer in convertible securities, Calamos launched one of the first convertible funds in 1985 and one of the first liquid alternative funds in 1990, reflecting a focus on innovation that continues to this day. Calamos Investments has grown into a global asset management firm with institutional and individual clients worldwide.

With more than 50 years of industry experience, he is often quoted as an authority on the markets and economy. He has authored two books on convertible securities.

Prior to entering the investment industry, Calamos served in the United States Air Force. His military career included five years of active duty flying B-52 bombers and 12 years in the reserves flying A-37 jet fighters. He retired with a rank of major.

Mr. Calamos received a BA in economics and an MBA in finance from Illinois Tech, where he established endowed chairs in philosophy and business and is also a member of the board of trustees.

John Catsimatidis

John Catsimatidis was born on the Greek Island of Nisyros in 1948 and six months later his parents emigrated to New York City. They settled in Harlem and his father found work as a busboy and his mother was a stay-at-home mom.

Catsimatidis earned his high school diploma from Brooklyn Tech. He studied electrical engineering at New York University while working in a small grocery store on nights and weekends to help his parents pay the bills. During his senior year, Catsimatidis dropped out of NYU to work in the grocery business full time. By the age of 25, he owned 10 Red Apple Supermarkets in Manhattan.

Now, four decades later, the Red Apple Group has evolved into a diversified corporation with holdings in the energy, aviation, retail, and real estate sectors and has over 8,000 employees.

Catsimatidis is a strong supporter of the Police Athletic League, serves on the board of Columbia Presbyterian Hospital, the Hellenic Times Scholarship Fund, and has held various volunteer positions in the Greek Orthodox Church.

Philip Christopher

Philip Christopher is president/CEO of American Network Solutions, which provides strategic consulting to companies in the telecommunications industry and beyond.

In his 30 years in the wireless industry, he has worked with every top carrier in the Americas and brought to the Americas Toshiba, Samsung, and Sharp, among others. He served as a member of the White House Economic Council and the CTIA Executive Board. Other boards he serves on include CTIA Wireless Foundation, New York Hospital Medical Center of Queens, Voxx International, and Atlantic Professional Soccer League.

He is the leader of the Greek Cypriot community and has dedicated his life to the struggle of Cypriots, including as founder and president of the Pancyprian Association of America and the International Coordinating Committee "Justice for Cyprus" (PSEKA).

He was the first Greek Cypriot to receive the Ellis Island Medal of Honor and is archon-lambadarios of the Order of Saint Andrew. He has been recognized by the Republic of Cyprus and others and is the recipient of keys to several cities including New York and San Francisco.

Congressman Charlie Crist

Charlie Crist represents Florida's 13th Congressional District in the US House of Representatives. The grandson of a Greek-Cypriot immigrant, Crist grew up in St. Petersburg, Florida, where he currently resides. He has spent his life's work serving his fellow Floridians. He was elected to the Florida Senate in 1992, as Florida's education commissioner in 2000, as Florida's attorney general in 2002 and as Florida's 44th governor in 2006. Through these positions, he focused on strengthening public education, environmental protections, voting rights, and civil rights. Crist was first elected to Congress in 2016, where he continues to work across the aisle to create jobs, increase wages, keep families safe, combat climate change, honor our veterans, protect the benefits seniors have earned, and always putting Florida first. He serves on the powerful House Appropriations Committee, as well as the Science, Space, and Technology Committee. Crist earned his bachelor's degree from Florida State University and his JD from Samford University Cumberland School of Law.

Antonis Diamataris

Antonis Diamataris was the publisher/editor of *Ethnikos Kirix*, the 106-year-old New York–based daily Greek language newspaper for over 40 years and founder, publisher/editor of its weekly English language sister publication, the *National Herald*, for over 25 years. He also served as a deputy foreign minister for the Greeks Abroad in the government of Kyriakos Mitsotakis.

Arthur Dimopoulos

Arthur Dimopoulos is executive director of the National Hellenic Society (NHS) and assisted in the establishment of the NHS's signature Heritage Greece Program. The program has sponsored 600+ college students of Greek descent that share a life-changing experience with students from the American College of Greece where they connect to their heritage, culture, roots, and Greek identity. Dimopoulos was of counsel at the K&L Gates law firm and served as an adjunct professor of law at Georgetown University Law Center where he received his Master of Laws degree with distinction. He received his Juris Doctorate degree at Southwestern Law in Los Angeles and completed undergraduate studies at Catholic University of America. Dimopoulos is the author of numerous published articles.

Michael Dukakis

Michael Dukakis served as governor of Massachusetts from 1975–1979 and again from 1983–1991. He is the longest serving governor in the state's history and only the second Greek American governor in US history. As well, Dukakis was the Democratic party's nominee for president in the 1988 election.

His father came to the US from Anatolia in 1912 and then proceeded to graduate from Harvard Medical School. His mother was born in Larissa and emigrated to the US at the age of nine from Vrysochori. She was one of the first young Greek women to ever go away to college and graduated Phi Beta Kappa from Bates College in 1925.

Dukakis is a graduate of Swarthmore College and then, following two years in the army, he attended and graduated from Harvard Law School. He recently retired from teaching at Northeastern University and UCLA.

Peter Economides

Peter Economides is a third generation Greek South African living in Greece.

He is a former executive vice president and worldwide director of client services at global advertising agency McCann Worldwide in New York—a position he reached after serving in senior management positions in South Africa, Hong Kong, Greece, and Mexico.

In 1996, he joined TBWA\Worldwide as head of global clients. A few years later he returned to his beloved Greece and established his own global brand consultancy, Felix BNI.

He has worked on some of the world's leading brands including American Express, Apple, Audi, Coca-Cola, General Motors, Heineken, The International Olympic Committee, Monaco Marine, Nestlé, Oceanco, and Unilever.

Economides is well known in Greece for encouraging Greek innovation, expressed in a single, powerful Greek word—*ΓΙΝΕΤΑΙ*!

He has been honoured with a Lifetime Achievement Award by the American Hellenic Council and a Members' Award of Excellence from the Propeller Club of the United States. His work has been recognised in three citations from the US Congress.

Mike Emanuel

Mike Emanuel currently serves as chief Washington correspondent for Fox News Channel (FNC). He joined FNC in 1997 as a Los Angeles-based correspondent.

Emanuel reported live from the Capitol as it was mobbed by rioters on January 6, 2021. Previously, Emanuel provided the latest breaking election news from Washington, DC, during FNC's Democracy 2020 election coverage. Additionally, Emanuel has covered both the House and Senate proceedings surrounding both impeachments of President Donald Trump, lawmakers passing tax reform, the confirmation hearings for the Trump and Biden cabinets, and the confirmation hearings for President Trump's three Supreme Court nominees.

Emanuel and his wife Evangeline met at a Greek Orthodox YAL Convention in Philadelphia in 2000. He and Evangeline were married at Saint George Greek Orthodox Church in Bethesda, Maryland, in 2002. They are the proud parents of son, Savas, and daughter, Tess.

Emanuel has served on the Parish Council of Saint George in Bethesda for the past 15 years. He was blessed and honored to become an archon of the Ecumenical Patriarchate in 2009.

Maria Foscarinis

Maria Foscarinis has advocated for solutions to homelessness in the United States since 1985. She is a primary architect of the landmark McKinney-Vento Act, the first major federal legislation addressing homelessness, and has led groundbreaking litigation to secure the legal rights of homeless persons. Foscarinis has published dozens of articles, book chapters, and opinion pieces; lectured widely; and been frequently quoted in the media.

In 1989, Foscarinis founded the National Homelessness Law Center (formerly known as the National Law Center on Homelessness & Poverty) and served as executive director until March 2021. She is a graduate of Columbia Law School, where she holds an adjunct appointment, teaching homelessness law and policy.

Recent awards include the 2016 Katharine and George Alexander Law Prize from Santa Clara University School of Law; in 2019, she was named a "Human Rights Hero" by the American Bar Association's *Human Rights* magazine. In 2021, she was a Rockefeller Foundation Practitioner Resident in Bellagio, Italy.

She is working on a book on homelessness and human rights.

Nicholas Gage

In his long career as a journalist, author, and producer, Nick Gage, who was born Nikos Gatzoyiannis in a remote mountain village in Epiros, has spent the first half of his life as an investigative reporter and foreign correspondent (the *New York Times*, the *Wall Street Journal*) and the second half writing seven books and producing several films, one of which was nominated for an Academy Award for best picture.

His books include *Greek Fire*, *A Place for Us*, and *Eleni*, his award-winning account of his mother's life and death during the Greek Civil War, which has been translated into 32 languages. "If *Eleni* were fiction, it would be the mark of genius," wrote the *New York Review of Books*.

He served as co-producer of the film *Eleni* and co-executive producer of *The Godfather: Part III*, which won an Oscar nomination for best picture in 1994. He has received five honorary degrees including a doctorate from Boston University.

He is married to the former Joan Paulson, also a writer, and they have three children: Christos, Eleni, and Marina.

John Georges

John Georges is the chairman and CEO of Georges Enterprises—a Louisiana-based organization that manages a diverse portfolio of companies including Imperial Trading, Georges Media, and more. Imperial Trading is one of the largest privately owned food distributors in the country. Georges Media oversees the operation of the *Times-Picayune* and Nola.com—the largest digital and print media outlet in the state of Louisiana. Georges is also a part owner of Galatoire's Restaurant. Not only is he committed to his home state, but he regularly visits his family in Greece.

He is the vice chairman of the National WWII Museum, a trustee at the Miller Center at the University of Virginia, and a member of the Friends of Saint Nicholas. Georges has also served on over 30 unique boards throughout his career.

Theodora (Dora) (Sideropoulos) Hancock

Theodora (Sideropoulos) Hancock (lt. colonel, USAF, ret.) co-founded the Hellenic American Women's Council.

She was a US Air Force officer for 20 years, served in Germany and Thailand, deployed to a war zone, is highly decorated—including the Bronze Star—and served three tours at the Pentagon, where she worked in International Acquisition, at the Office of the Secretary of Defense. She was knighted by the Sovereign Military Order of the Temple of Jerusalem (Templars).

She founded Hancock International, an international defense consulting company. Clients included the Greek Ministry of Defense and the Finnish Foreign Trade Office.

After September 11, she worked for the intelligence community and then returned to the Pentagon and served on a congressionally mandated Panel on Intellectual Property and Technical Data Rights.

She has a BA in linguistics, MBA in economics and finance; post-graduate work includes three senior professional military schools and law and acquisition courses.

She serves on the boards of various companies and nonprofit organizations, speaks Greek fluently, and is active in the Greek American community.

Kelly Vlahakis-Hanks

Kelly Vlahakis-Hanks is president and CEO of Earth Friendly Products°, maker of ECOS° plant-powered laundry detergents and cleaners that are safer for people, pets, and the planet.

Vlahakis-Hanks has led ECOS to become the first company in the world to achieve carbon neutrality, water neutrality, and TRUE Platinum Zero Waste certification. ECOS has received many awards for its innovations in green chemistry, including the US EPA's Safer Choice Partner of the Year.

Under her leadership, ECOS offers one of the strongest employee benefits programs in the industry, including medical insurance, paid leave, and wellness programs. As a woman of Greek and African

American heritage, she has created a corporate culture of diversity and empowerment, and 63 percent of her top executives are women.

Vlahakis-Hanks has received many awards for her sustainable leadership, including *Entrepreneur* magazine's 100 Powerful Women in 2020 and Conscious Company's World-Changing Women in Conscious Business. She is an active member of several boards, including the XPRIZE Foundation, and she is active in public policy advocacy to protect human health and the environment.

Menas C. Kafatos

Menas C. Kafatos is the Fletcher Jones Endowed Chair Professor of Computational Physics at Chapman University and Director of the Center of Excellence in Earth Systems Modeling and Observations (CEESMO). As founding dean of the Schmid College of Science and Technology and vice chancellor at Chapman, he promoted and established interdisciplinary educational and research projects and, subsequently as director of CEESMO, is leading many science grants.

Author, physicist, and philosopher, he works in quantum mechanics, cosmology, the environment, climate change, and natural hazards, and extensively on philosophical issues of consciousness, connecting science to metaphysical traditions. He leads collaborations of his research teams with several universities and international institutions and holds seminars and workshops on the universal principles for well-being and human potential.

He works extensively and leads projects in all areas of hazards: wildfires, droughts, dust transport, hurricane modeling, as well as impacts of climate change on agriculture and natural ecosystems.

He is the author of hundreds of articles and book chapters and is the author or editor of 21 books.

Father Alexander (Alex) Karloutsos

Father Alexander Karloutsos is the Protopresbyter of the Ecumenical Patriarchate as well as the pastor of the Dormition of the Virgin Mary Church of the Hamptons.

He is the former vicar general of the Greek Orthodox Archdiocese of America where he served as the Archdiocesan liaison to the White House, the Congress, state and local officials, Greek American organizations, political action, religious freedom, and human rights groups.

He is also the Spiritual Advisor to the Order of Saint Andrew and Friends of Saint Nicholas National Shrine at the World Trade Center.

In 2022, he received the Presidential Medal of Freedom, the nation's highest civilian honor. As President Joe Biden said, he is "a humble servant of God and...through more than 50 years of service with moral clarity, love of family and pride in the Greek American community, the man known simply as Father Alex to Presidents and parishioners alike, inspires us to believe in the power of 'We the People.'"

He is married to Xanthi Karavellas Karloutsos. They have three children, happily married, and nine grandchildren, Alexander, Konstantine, Xanthi, Luca, Konstantina, Demetrios, Steven, Leo and Michael, Jr.

Peter Karmanos Jr.

Peter Karmanos is the current chairman of MadDog Technology, a high-tech venture capital firm, and several MadDog portfolio companies, including Resolute Building Intelligence, Lenderful, LenderAuto, Freight Verify, Shapelog, and MadDog Professional Services; also, MadDog Ventures Fund Manager and General Partner.

Until recently, he was owner and then minority owner for the Carolina Hurricanes. Having been involved in hockey for over 40 years, Karmanos was inducted into the Hockey Hall of Fame in 2015. He remains the driving force behind the Compuware youth hockey program.

He established the Barbara Ann Karmanos Cancer Institute in Detroit and he and his wife, Danialle, are involved in numerous other philanthropic endeavors as well.

Jimmy Kokotas

Jimmy Kokotas serves as supreme president of the American Hellenic Educational Progressive Association (AHEPA).

As well, Kokotas serves as an archon of the Ecumenical Patriarchate; member of Leadership 100; member of the Parish Council, Saint Nicholas Church and National Shrine; board member of Saint Photios Greek Orthodox National Shrine; and co-chair, Three Hierarchs Church Audit Committee.

Tom Korologos

Tom C. Korologos, a former United States ambassador to Belgium, served with the Coalition Provisional Authority in Iraq and has been an advisor to five United States presidents. A native of Salt Lake City, Utah, he was an altar boy at the Greek Orthodox Church and also chairman of the Board of Trustees of the American College of Greece. He graduated from the University of Utah, worked at the *Salt Lake Tribune*, the Associated Press, and the *New York Herald Tribune* and received Grantland Rice and Pulitzer Traveling Fellowships from the Columbia University Graduate School of Journalism. He served on the staff of Utah senator Wallace F. Bennett and at the White House in the Nixon/Ford administrations. He is former chairman of the Advisory Commission on Public Diplomacy, was on the US Broadcasting Board of Governors, and a member of the Advisory Board of the National Security Agency. He also was a vice president at Timmons and Co., the Washington, DC, consulting firm. He is a strategic advisor at DLA Piper. He has assisted in the US Senate confirmation for more than 300 persons including Supreme Court justices and cabinet members. He is married to Ann McLaughlin, former secretary of labor in the Reagan administration.

Eleni Kounalakis

Ambassador Eleni Kounalakis was sworn in as the 50th lieutenant governor of California by Governor Gavin Newsom on January 7, 2019. She is the first woman elected to the post. From 2010 to 2013, Kounalakis served as US ambassador to the Republic of Hungary and in 2015 published her acclaimed memoir, *Madam Ambassador, Three Years of Diplomacy, Dinner Parties and Democracy in Budapest* (The New Press). Prior to her service, Kounalakis spent 18 years as an executive at one of California's most respected housing development firms, AKT Development. Throughout her career, she served on numerous boards and commissions including California's First 5 Commission, the San Francisco War Memorial, San Francisco Port Commission, and the Association of American Ambassadors. Kounalakis graduated from Dartmouth College in 1989, earned her MBA from UC Berkeley's Haas School of Business in 1992, and holds an honorary Doctor of Laws degree from the American College of Greece. She is married to Dr. Markos Kounalakis and the couple has two teenage sons, Neo and Eon.

Stamatios M. (Tom) Krimigis

Dr. Stamatios Krimigis is emeritus head of the Space Exploration Sector at the Johns Hopkins Applied Physics Laboratory (APL), a member of the Academy of Athens, has built instruments that have flown to all nine classical planets beginning with Mariner 4 to Mars in 1965, and is principal investigator on NASA's Voyager 1, 2. In 1999 the International Astronomical Union named asteroid 1979 UH as 8323 Krimigis. Among his most recent awards are the Smithsonian National Air and Space Museum Trophy for Lifetime Achievement (2015), the NASA Distinguished Public Service Medal (2016), and the Theodore von Karman Award (2017) of the International Academy of Astronautics. He has published more than 630 papers in peer-reviewed journals and books, is a fellow of the American

Geophysical Union, American Physical Society, American Institute of Aeronautics and Astronautics, American Association for the Advancement of Science, and was honored by a special resolution of the US Senate "for exceptional contributions to space science" (2018).

Niki Leondakis

CorePower Yoga CEO, Niki Leondakis, has consistently built and led some of the most diverse and customer-centric teams in the hospitality industry. She has more than 30 years of experience building lifestyle brands and creating award-winning workplace cultures that drive innovation, and employee and customer loyalty. Leondakis has served as CEO of multiple companies including Equinox Fitness Clubs, Two Roads Hospitality, and Commune Hotels & Resorts, as well as president of Kimpton Hotels and Restaurants. Leondakis also serves on the Board of Directors of The RealReal, Inc. (REAL) and the board of Dress for Success Worldwide since 2005, including service as chair of the board. In addition to receiving awards from various publications for innovation, creating great places to work, being a CEO Trailblazer, and a Lifetime Achievement Award Winner, she was named one of the 100 Most Influential Women by the *San Francisco Business Times* regularly since 2002.

Anthony J. Limberakis, MD

Anthony J. Limberakis, MD, is a radiologist based in Philadelphia, Pennsylvania, with his wife, Dr. Maria, and three children and four grandchildren. He currently serves as national commander of the Order of Saint Andrew and chair of the Ecumenical Patriarch Bartholomew Foundation. Previously he served as president of the Duke University School of Medicine Alumni Association, president of the Duke University Davison Club, and a member of the Duke University Medical Center Board of Visitors. He has received numerous recognitions for his efforts in the arena of human rights including the Athenagoras Human Rights Award, the Ellis Island Medal of Honor, and an honorary Doctorate degree in humanities from Hellenic College. He is a Distinguished Fellow of the Oxford Centre for the Study of Law and Public Policy at Harris Manchester College of the University of Oxford and has received numerous recognitions from Duke University including the Charles Duke Award and the Distinguished Service Award. He is a fulfilled member of Leadership 100 and currently serves on the academic faculty of Thomas Jefferson Medical School.

George M. Logothetis

George Logothetis is the Chairman and CEO of Libra Group, a privately-owned, international business group. Owned by the Logothetis family, Libra Group began with one subsidiary and has grown into a network of industries and activities with assets and operations in nearly 60 countries. Within its ecosystem of 20 businesses and ten social initiatives—the Group is driven to achieve balance among growth and good, twin engines that move it forward.

The Group's primary holdings include aviation, energy, maritime, real estate, and hospitality while maintaining and developing interests in other sectors. The Group supports a wide range of social responsibility programs including internships, fellowships, backing for entrepreneurs, refugee aid, and support for charitable and other non-profit organizations. George and his wife Nitzia are founders of the Seleni Institute, a New York-based non-profit that addresses maternal mental health with the simple insight, "Change a mother's life, change a child's life." George is also Chairman of the non-profit Leadership Council of Concordia, which promotes public-private partnerships, and is a member of the Board of Directors of President Barack Obama's My Brother's Keeper (MBK) Alliance.

Maria Loi

Chef Maria Loi is an internationally renowned entrepreneur, author, television personality, and philanthropist working to change the world—one healthy bite at a time. Known as the Julia Child of Greece, she is the founder and face of a lifestyle brand which nurtures a healthy body and soul, melds the inspiration of ancient Greece with a modern approach to the Mediterranean diet, and helps people boost their immunity and improve their health, wellness, and longevity.

The founder of Loi Food Products, and namesake of Loi Estiatorio in Manhattan, Loi has cooked for celebrities and presidents.

The author of over 36 cookbooks and magazines, she is host of a new show, *The Life of Loi*, on PBS, which debuted in 2021. It aims to build an inspirational and educational movement around the Mediterranean diet and lifestyle—from ancient to modern, food to culture, and everything in between.

Named Ambassador of Greek Gastronomy by the Chef's Club of Greece, Loi is also a passionate philanthropist supporting a wide variety of causes focused on children and the underserved.

Congresswoman Nicole Malliotakis

Congresswoman Malliotakis represents the 11th Congressional District of New York, encompassing Staten Island and Southern Brooklyn. The daughter of immigrants, her father is from Greece and her mother from Cuba.

Prior to serving in Congress, Malliotakis worked as Community Liaison for former New York Governor George Pataki, and a Public Affairs Manager for Con Edison. Malliotakis was elected to the New York State Assembly in 2010 where she was the first Greek American woman elected to the State Legislature and the first Hispanic elected on Staten Island. Currently, Malliotakis is the only Republican representing New York City on the federal level.

Mike A. Manatos, President of Manatos & Manatos

Mike Manatos, President of Manatos & Manatos, is building on his family's legacy as one of the most trusted and established in Washington, DC. He is the 3rd generation of Manatoses to specialize in the areas of public policy, government relations, strategic consulting and advocacy, and has done so successfully for over 32 years. Dubbed "lobbying royalty" by *US News & World Report*, the Manatos family has been working with top US policy makers, both Republicans and Democrats, formulating US policy for over 86 years and has a respected record of consistently opening doors at the highest levels throughout Washington, DC.

Manatos has served as Executive Director of the Washington Oxi Day Foundation since 2011 and serves on the board/leadership of the top national Greek American organizations, including Leadership 100 (Executive Board), National Hellenic Society (Executive Board), Greek Orthodox Archdiocese of America (Archdiocesan Council), Archons of the Ecumenical Patriarchate (Government Affairs Committee Chair), and the National Hellenic Students Association (Advisory Board).

John G. Manos

John G. Manos is president of Bank Financial, specializing in commercial real estate lending nationally. In addition to being a banker, he is a registered architect with professional experience in the development of commercial, residential and multifamily projects.

Manos, full name Manoukarakis, was born in Rethymno, Crete, Greece, and in 1967 immigrated to the US with his family to settle in Chicago.

Manos is a former president in the Pancretan Association of America, past president and chairman of the United Hellenic Voters of America, an archon of the Order of Saint Andrew the Apostle, a member of Leadership 100, and a recipient of the Ellis Island Medal of Honor.

George M. Marcus

George M. Marcus is the founder of Marcus & Millichap and its chairman since 1971. Marcus & Millichap is the parent company of a diversified group of real estate, service, investment, and development firms including SummerHill Homes, one of the San Francisco Bay Area's largest home builders. Also falling under the Marcus & Millichap family of companies are Pacific Urban Residential, SummerHill Apartment Communities, Meridian Property Company, and Hanover Real Estate Investors. Marcus is also founder and chairman of Essex Property Trust (ESS) and Marcus & Millichap, Inc. (MMI), both publicly traded companies. He was one of the original founders and directors of Plaza Commerce Bank and the Greater Bay Bancorp; he is a regent emeritus of the University of California; he's a member of the Real Estate Roundtable and the Policy Advisory Board of the University of California at Berkeley Fisher Center for Real Estate and Urban Economics, among others. He is chairman emeritus of the National Hellenic Society.

A major philanthropist, Marcus was born in Euboea, Greece, and migrated to the US with his family in 1945, at the age of four.

Dennis Mehiel

Dennis Mehiel, a New York City native, enjoyed a long career in the packaging industry, having twice built America's largest independent manufacturer of corrugated boxes. His philanthropic activities have been focused on educational support, serving for 10 years as a trustee of the Purnell School in Pottersville, New Jersey; for five years as a trustee of the Windward School in White Plains, New York; and was the first person not of the Jewish faith elected to the Board of Governors of Yeshiva University's Wurzweiler School of Social Work.

Mehiel's civic engagement includes service as vice chair of the Empire State Development Corporation, a member of the New York City Campaign Finance Board, and as the chairman and CEO of the Battery Park City Authority. Mehiel currently serves as the chairman of Friends of Saint Nicholas, charged with building the

Saint Nicholas National Shrine at Ground Zero in lower Manhattan. The Shrine replaces the Saint Nicholas Greek Orthodox Church, the only house of worship destroyed when the World Trade Center was attacked on 9/11.

C. Dean Metropoulos

C. Dean Metropoulos is an investor, businessman, and major philanthropist. He is chairman and CEO of Metropoulos & Co., a boutique acquisition and management firm. Metropoulos, with his two sons, Evan and Daren, have spent the past 35+ years building, restructuring, and growing numerous businesses in the US, Mexico, and Europe. Many of these were subsequently taken public or sold to strategic corporations.

Metropoulos has been involved in more than 87 acquisitions and five SPACs involving over $56 billion in invested capital and has earned some of the most attractive returns on Wall Street. Highly respected for his integrity and commitment, Metropoulos is a sought-after partner by many of the major private equity firms.

Metropoulos holds a bachelor's and MBA from Babson College and enrolled at Columbia University for postgraduate studies, prior to moving to Europe as the youngest corporate CFO for Europe, Middle East, and Africa for GTE International.

Metropoulos and his wife, Marianne, of 45 years, reside in Palm Beach, Florida.

John Negroponte

Ambassador Negroponte is vice chairman of McLarty Associates. Previously he held government positions abroad and in Washington between 1960 and 1997 and again from 2001 to 2008.

He has been ambassador to Honduras, Mexico, the Philippines, the United Nations, and Iraq. In Washington he served twice on the National Security Council staff, first as director for Vietnam in the Nixon administration and then as deputy national security advisor under President Reagan. He has also held a cabinet level position as the first director of national intelligence under President George W. Bush. His most recent position in government was as deputy secretary of state, where he served as the State Department's chief operating officer. From 1975 to 1977, Negroponte was United States consul general in Thessaloniki, Greece.

Congressman Chris Pappas

Congressman Chris Pappas was first elected in 2018 to represent the 1st Congressional District of the state of New Hampshire.

A lifelong resident of Manchester, New Hampshire, Pappas was born into a proud Greek American family. After graduating from Harvard, Pappas returned home where he began a career in public service while helping run the 105-year-old family restaurant where he started scooping ice cream and bussing tables at the age of 14.

John A. Payiavlas

John A. Payiavlas is founder and chairman of AVI Foodsystems. He was born to Greek immigrants, Anthony and Paraskevi, in 1931 in Warren, Ohio. He is a veteran of the Korean War and recipient of the Commander's Cross of Valour from Greece.

After service, John returned home and purchased a small vending company in 1960. He worked diligently to grow the business, while he and his wife, Marisa, raised their two children, Patrice and Anthony.

Renamed AVI Foodsystems in 1987, the company serves 7,000 locations in 44 states. Payiavlas attributes his company's success to great food, a family atmosphere, and strong relationships. Giving back is important to his philosophy. He is a member of St. Demetrios Greek Orthodox Church (Warren), chairman emeritus of Leadership 100; served as council member of Greek Orthodox Archdiocesan Council Executive Committee; and an archon depoutatos of the Ecumenical Patriarchate. Payiavlas received the Ellis Island Medal of Honor; Northeast Ohio Business Hall of Fame induction; and the

Cleveland Clinic's Distinguished Fellow Award. He remains very involved with his family, business, and community.

James (Jim) Pedas and Theodore (Ted) Pedas

While attending George Washington University Law School, brothers Jim and Ted Pedas established a recording company and also became involved in the movie business. They started with three drive-in movie theatres and expanded to almost 100 screens in the Washington, DC area known as the Circle/Showcase theatre circuit.

In 1984, the Pedas brothers formed Circle Releasing Corporation and later Circle Films, devoted to the distribution of foreign and art films. They distributed *Blood Simple*, the first of many films they produced for Joel and Ethan Coen.

The Pedas brothers formed Circle Management Company to oversee their real estate investments, including the co-development of the 700,000-square-foot Rio Washingtonian Center in Maryland.

The Pedas brothers are the recipients of numerous awards for their work in promoting motion pictures as an art form, including Washingtonians of the Year and the American University's Award for Contribution to Film Culture. Jim Pedas also received an honorary doctorate from Thiel College and Ted Pedas received the Joseph Wharton Award, Wharton School of Business, and the NATO Marquee Award, among others. They are both archons of the Ecumenical Patriarchate with the Order of Saint Andrew the Apostle and long-standing members of The Archbishop Iakovos Leadership 100 Fund, Inc. As well, they have supported many philanthropic endeavors, including funding an Intellectual Property Chair at George Washington University Law School.

Paulette Poulos

Paulette Poulos is executive director of The Archbishop Iakovos Leadership 100 Fund, Inc., a leading charitable membership organization, whose purpose is to support the Greek Orthodox Church in America and advance Orthodoxy and Hellenism. She was appointed to Leadership 100 as director of development in 2005, ultimately being named executive director in 2011. Her career spans some 55 years of executive leadership, financial development, philanthropy, church, and community service. His Eminence Archbishop Elpidophoros appointed her to a newly established advisory committee, "Senators for Orthodoxy and Hellenism."

Beginning in 1965 with the Department of Laity of the Greek Orthodox Archdiocese of America, she moved rapidly to become associate director of youth ministry in 1970, director of LOGOS, and administrator for the late Archbishop Iakovos, serving from 1984 to 2005 upon his passing. Throughout her years of service, Poulos has been a strong advocate and supporter for the clergy.

Poulos is credited with having raised significant funds for Hellenic College/Holy Cross School of Theology, the Archbishop Iakovos Library and Learning Resource Center, and Leadership 100.

Michael Psaros

Michael Psaros is a co-founder and co-managing partner of KPS Capital Partners, LP, a leading global private equity firm with approximately $13.4 billion of assets under management. Psaros is an Archon of the Order of Saint Andrew, where he serves on its National Council and is a trustee of the Ecumenical Patriarch Bartholomew Foundation. He is a founding member of FAITH: An Endowment for Orthodoxy and Hellenism, a trustee of Leadership 100, and serves on the Executive Board of The Hellenic Initiative. He is the Chairman of Friends of Saint Nicholas, the organization responsible for constructing the St. Nicholas Shrine at Ground Zero. He previously served as the Treasurer of the Greek Orthodox Archdiocese of America. Psaros serves on the Board of Directors of Georgetown University and as Vice Chairman of the Board of Advisors of Georgetown's McDonough School of Business. Psaros and his family created and endowed "The Psaros Center for Financial Markets and Policy at Georgetown University" in 2022, "The Ecumenical Patriarch Bartholomew Endowed Orthodox Chaplaincy, Endowed by the Michael Psaros Family" in 2021, and "The Michael and Robin Psaros Endowed Chair in Business Administration" at Georgetown's McDonough School in 2013.

Jeannie Ranglas

Jeannie Ranglas, born and raised in Chicago, Illinois, to parents of Greek ancestry, moved to San Diego when she married Gerry in 1978. As of 2022, she is currently in her 12th year as the Metropolis of San Francisco Philoptochos president. She has also been a member of the National Philoptochos Board for the Archdiocese for 20 years, currently serving as first vice president.

Ranglas has been recognized by a number of organizations for her community service and leadership.

She and her husband Gerry are members of Leadership 100 and are benefactors of the Metropolis of San Francisco, the Ecumenical Patriarchate, and the Archdiocese, among others. They were also founders of their parish of Saints Constantine and Helen Greek Orthodox Church in Cardiff-by-the-Sea, California.

They are the lead donors for the establishment of the Gerry and Jeannie Ranglas Endowed Chair in Ancient Greek History at the University of California, San Diego.

They have two children, Athan Ranglas and Alexis Ranglas-Behseta (Romin Behseta), and are the proud grandparents of Juliette Evangelia.

Congressman John Sarbanes

Congressman Sarbanes has represented the 3rd Congressional District of Maryland since 2007. He has led efforts in the US House of Representatives to pass HR1, the For the People Act, a historic suite of reforms to protect and expand the right to vote, clean up corruption in Washington, and restore trust, transparency and integrity in government. Born and raised in Baltimore, he graduated from Princeton University and studied law and politics in Greece on a Fulbright Scholarship before attending Harvard Law School. He is the eldest son of the late Senator Paul Sarbanes.

Dean A. Spanos

Dean Spanos is controlling owner and chairman of the board of the Los Angeles Chargers, providing senior leadership, strategic direction, and critical resources as the Chargers continue writing an exciting new chapter in their storied history. Spanos also serves as president of the A.G. Spanos Companies, where along with his brother Michael, he oversees all construction operations for the family's business nationwide.

As a member of the NFL's Management Council Executive Committee, Spanos plays an integral role in negotiating the NFL's labor agreements and as a member, and former chair, of the NFL's Business Ventures Committee, he oversees the league's commercial activities, including consumer products, sponsorship, events, marketing, and new business initiatives.

Dean, his wife, Susie, and his entire family have a multigenerational commitment to community involvement and are recognized as one of the NFL's most philanthropic families. Their financial contributions of tens of millions of dollars and their emotional support for youth, sports, education, and our brave men and women in uniform have been a hallmark of their team ownership and legacy.

Commissioner Mariyana T. Spyropoulos

Mariyana Spyropoulos was first elected to the Board of Commissioners of the Metropolitan Water Reclamation District (MWRD) of Greater Chicago in 2010. She has her law degree from the University of Illinois Chicago School of Law and MBA from Loyola University Chicago. She served as MWRD's chairperson of finance (2013–2015) and president of the board of commissioners (2015–2019). She serves as chairperson of the Judiciary and of the Pension, Human Resources, and Civil Service Committees. Spyropoulos has ensured that MWRD maintains its AAA bond rating and balanced annual budget. In addition, she has advocated for policies that support investing in infrastructure, protecting our water environment, sustainability, and fighting climate change. She is the daughter of immigrants. Her father was from Kalavryta, Greece. Spyropoulos is a member of the Chicago Sierra Club, the Hellenic Bar Association, Women's Bar Association, and Sankofa House Board. She received the 2017 Illinois Water Environment Association Public Service Award and in 2021, the Public Officials Award from the Water Environment Federation.

James George Stavridis

James Stavridis is a retired United States Navy admiral and best-selling author. He was the 16th Supreme Allied Commander at NATO. He currently serves as vice chair, Global Affairs and managing director of the global investment firm the Carlyle Group and chair of the Board of Trustees of the Rockefeller Foundation. His novel, *2034: A Novel of the Next World War*, was co-written with Elliot Ackerman and published in March 2021. It debuted at #6 on the *New York Times* Best Seller list.

Previously, Stavridis served as the dean of the Fletcher School of Law and Diplomacy at Tufts University, where he earned a PhD.

Stavridis serves as the chief international diplomacy and national security analyst for NBC News and contributing editor of *Time* magazine.

Athan Stephanopoulos

Athan Stephanopoulos is president of NowThis, the leading digital media brand that produces and distributes video news content for an audience that lives at the intersection of mobile and social. Stephanopoulos oversees all business operations of the company—editorial, product strategy, publishing, brand partnerships, and data insights. Since joining in 2014, Stephanopoulos has been at the helm of NowThis as it became the pioneer in the distributed media model—producing video content consumed natively across all social platforms. NowThis is the largest news source for Millennials and Gen-Z globally, with a monthly U.S. reach of more than 60 percent of all people in their 20s, and billions of monthly video views across all its digital channels.

Previously, Stephanopoulos was founder and CEO of Cliptamatic, a social video distribution platform acquired by NowThis in 2014. The company boasted an impressive list of media companies who utilized the platform to distribute videos across social media—including Paramount Pictures, HBO, ABC News, AMC Networks, and MTV. Stephanopoulos has served as an adjunct professor at Fordham University's Graduate School of Business in New York City and is a member of the Council on Foreign Relations. He resides in New York City with his wife and two children.

George Stephanopoulos

George Stephanopoulos is anchor of ABC's *Good Morning America* and *This Week with George Stephanopoulos.*

He has conducted interviews with a wide range of subjects including world leaders such as Presidents Joe Biden, Donald Trump, and Barack Obama; Israeli Prime Minister Benjamin Netanyahu; Iranian President Mahmoud Ahmadinejad; and Russian President Vladimir Putin. He has interviewed celebrities, politicians, and business leaders including George Clooney, Rep. Nancy Pelosi, Billy Porter, Facebook CEO Mark Zuckerberg, former FBI Director James Comey, and more. Stephanopoulos has led the network's coverage of four presidential elections and he moderated live town hall events with former President Donald Trump in 2016 and 2020 and then-presidential candidate Joe Biden in 2020.

Prior to joining ABC News, he served in the Clinton administration as the senior advisor to the president for policy and strategy. He is the author of *All Too Human*, a *New York Times* best seller.

Congresswoman Dina Titus

Dina Titus represents Nevada's 1st District in the US House of Representatives. Titus graduated from William and Mary and received her PhD from Florida State University in 1977. She taught American government at UNLV from 1977–2012. She was minority leader of the Nevada State Senate from 1991 to 2008 when she was first elected to Congress.

Titus is a proud Greek American who considers her Hellenic background an important part of her personal and political life. She took her oath of office with her hand on her grandfather's Greek Bible.

Titus serves on the House Foreign Affairs, Transportation and Infrastructure, and Homeland Security Committees. She is a member of the Hellenic and Greek-Israel Caucus. She strongly supports efforts to protect the Ecumenical Patriarchate in Istanbul, reunify Cyprus, and return the Pantheon marbles. She represented President Obama at the opening of the Acropolis Museum in Athens and has been privileged to meet with His All-Holiness Bartholomew on a number of occasions. She has received the Pericles Award from the American Hellenic Council and been honored by PSEKA and the Daughters of Penelope.

Angelo K. Tsakopoulos

Tsakopoulos is a Greek American businessman, real estate developer, and philanthropist. He is the Founder of AKT Development.

George James Tsunis

George Tsunis is the son of first-generation immigrants from Nafoaktos, Greece, James and Eleni Tsunis. He was born in Queens, New York, and received his BA from New York University and his law degree from St. John's University School of Law.

Tsunis is the founder, chairman, and CEO of Chartwell Hotels and former partner at the law firm Rivkin Radler. He currently serves as U.S. Ambassador to Greece. The views expressed in his remarks are his own and not necessarily those of the U.S. government. He has been involved in major institutions in the Greek American community, including the Archdiocesan Council of the Greek Orthodox Archdiocese of America, the Faith and Leadership 100 Endowments, the Hellenic American Leadership Council (HALC), and The Hellenic Initiative.

Former Archbishop Demetrios awarded Tsunis the Saint Paul's Medal, the Greek Orthodox Church of America's highest recognition for a layperson. Tsunis has also received the Federation of Cypriot American Organizations "Justice for Cyprus" Award—bestowed on him by former Cypriot President Dimitris Christofias, and the joint American Jewish Committee/HALC Athens-Wishner Award.

Argyris (R.J.) Vassiliou

Argyris (R.J.) Vassiliou is president of two family-owned businesses, Acme Pallet Company, an industrial engineering concern, and Di-Cor Industries, a specialty structural steel fabrication company.

Vassiliou received his BCE degree from The Cooper Union for the Advancement of Science and Art, and a master's from Princeton University. He is a member of Tau Beta Pi, the National Engineering Honor Society, and Chi Epsilon, the National Civil Engineering Honor Society.

Vassiliou is the immediate past chairman of The Archbishop Iakovos Leadership 100 Fund, Inc., is an Executive Committee board member of Anatolia College in Thessaloniki, Greece, and sits on the President's Advisory Council of Mitchell College and the Parents

Council of Skidmore College. He also serves on the Advisory Council of the Princeton University Art Museum, the Frances Young Tang Teaching Museum and Art Gallery at Skidmore College, and on the board of the John and Mary Pappajohn Scholarship Foundation.

Fluent in Greek, he is a recipient of the Ellis Island Medal of Honor. He and his wife, the former Ann Pappajohn, have two children.

Emmanuel E. Velivasakis

Emmanuel E. Velivasakis is a widely acclaimed structural engineer and served as president of the Pancretan Association of America.

Born on the island of Crete, Velivasakis received his primary and secondary education in Greece. After serving in the Greek Army, he came to the United States where he received his bachelor's and master's degrees in civil/structural engineering from the City College of the City University of New York.

Velivasakis served as managing principal of Thornton-Tomasetti, an internationally acclaimed architectural-engineering design firm and president of its LZA Technology Division.

His design firm has completed the structural design of several high-rise buildings in Asia, Europe, and the US, including the soon-to-be world's tallest 1001-meters-tall Jeddah Tower in Saudi Arabia.

In 1997, the Architect of the Capitol selected Velivasakis' design firm to lead the effort for the evaluation and restoration design of the Dome of the Capitol building in Washington, DC. As well, his firm is a member of the Santiago Calatrava's Design Team for the Saint Nicholas Shrine at Ground Zero.

Acknowledgements

I am particularly indebted to His Eminence Archbishop Elpidophoros of America who opened the book's second section and to the 57 extraordinarily successful Hellenes who took the time from their pressing schedules to contribute their thoughts about Hellenism in their lives that are included in that second section.

I would like to thank some individuals whose review and numerous edits to my text were particularly helpful: Matthew Cooper and my wife, Tina.

I am indebted to Aliki Theofilopoulos for her contribution of numerous original sketches.

As well, I appreciate those who took the time to read the text and let me know if it seemed to be headed in the right direction: Dr. Mike Datch, Leon Andris, Mark Arey, Father Alex Karloutsos, Peter Poulos, and Vanessa Andris who also expressed the perfect summary of the hope for Hellenism and is included in the conclusion of the book.

I must also express my appreciation to experts such as Dr. Artemis Simopoulos, Professor Polyvia' Parara, and Zoie Lafis for their helpful input.

And a special thanks to Manatos & Manatos and particularly Kimberley Matthews Fraser, whose hundreds of hours of hard work and insights made the coming together of this book possible.

About the Author

Andy Manatos, CEO of Manatos and Manatos, a firm he originally established with his father, has spent over a half-century in the field of public policy in Washington, D.C. His experience includes his time as the youngest Presidential advance man for President Lyndon Johnson, the youngest U.S. Senate Committee Staff Director, and the youngest Assistant Secretary in the Carter Administration.

He was selected as one of the 100 most influential people in private sector Washington by *Regardies Magazine*. *The National Journal* said, "his style is that of a Washington insider."

Andy led the legislative fight that invoked cloture in the U.S. Senate for only the 17th time in history, created an annual meeting with each President of the United States for every year for over 30 years, created the only award presented by the U.S. Senate, and created the only White House Conference allowed by one administration, among other accomplishments.

Andy played a significant role in the creation of a grassroots lobby that has been described by Presidents as one of the most powerful in America. In addition, he created and subsidized a not-for-profit organization that distributed free to high schools across America over 360,000 award-winning, civic educational videos viewed by over 30 million students. He raised over $1.5 million per year for these award-winning videos that featured nationally known figures such as former Secretary of State Colin Powell; Ambassador Caroline Kennedy, daughter of President John Kennedy; the late Supreme Court Justice Ruth Bader Ginsburg; among many other nationally and internationally known figures.

He has been a guest op-ed writer for *The Washington Post, The New York Times, The Chicago Tribune* and other newspapers.

A life-long member of the Greek Orthodox Church, he was appointed a member and Regional Leader of the Order of St. Andrew. He also is a member of the Greek Archdiocesan Council and Senator. He serves with President Bill Clinton on the board of the THEA Foundation.

Awards he has received include:

- Medal of Saint Paul, the highest recognition of the Greek Orthodox Church of America (2008)
- Ellis Island Medal of Honor from the National Ethnic Coalition of Organizations (1999)
- Lifetime Achievement at the Greek America Foundation's Gabby Awards at Carnegie Hall in New York City (2017)
- Lifetime Achievement Award by the Alpha Omega Council in Boston, MA (2016)
- Venizelon Award from the Pancretan Association of America (2019)
- Battle of Crete Award from the Pancretan Association of America (1991)
- Outstanding Public Advocacy Award from the American Hellenic Educational and Progressive Association (AHEPA) (2013)
- Service Award from The Smile of the Child Foundation in Athens, Greece (2013)

Born in Washington, D.C., Andy has lived in the D.C. area all of his life. He is married to Tina Manatos. They have four adult sons — Mike (Laura), Nick (Despina), Tom (Dana) and George — and eight grandchildren.

The Washington Oxi Day Foundation

Founded in 2011, the Washington Oxi Day Foundation is a nonprofit, 501c3 organization dedicated to informing American policymakers, world leaders and the public about the profound role Greece played in defying Hitler's Axis Forces and bringing about the eventual outcome of World War II. Today, the Foundation celebrates modern day heroes fighting to preserve freedom and promote democracy in the spirit of the Greeks.

The Foundation's annual Oxi Courage Awards take place in Washington, DC, on or around October 28, Oxi Day in Greece. It brings together senior US officials and other international leaders with influential Washingtonians, human rights activists, and others along with prominent Greek Americans. Notable individuals who have submitted nominations for the Foundation's awards include former President Bill Clinton, singer-songwriter Bono, and human rights attorney Amal Clooney.

Previous Oxi Courage honorees include remarkable individuals who have gone on to win the Nobel Peace Prize, including journalist Maria Ressa (2019), and survivor of ISIS atrocities Nadia Murad (2016), as well as twice-poisoned Russian democracy activist Vladimir Kara-Murza (2018).

The Foundation also presents an annual Metropolitan Chrysostomos Award, named after the brave religious leader on Zakynthos who offered to sacrifice himself to save the island's Jewish population during the Holocaust. Previous recipients of this prestigious honor include His All-Holiness Ecumenical Patriarch Bartholomew (2021), the late civil rights icon Congressman John Lewis (2020), former president of Israel Shimon Peres (2014), Nobel laureate and Holocaust survivor Elie Wiesel (2012), and the mother of Queen Elizabeth's late husband Prince Philip, Princess Alice (2015), who shielded a Jewish family in her home in Nazi-occupied Athens across from a Gestapo office at the height of WWII.

The Foundation also celebrates and honors the courage of those who defended their country in WWII, the Korean War, and the Vietnam War at a moving ceremony at the national WWII Memorial.

In addition, the Foundation resurrected the uniquely Greek word *"philotimo"* with a powerful short film that has been viewed by millions worldwide and holds an annual *philotimo* scholarship competition for Greek American high school students.

1100 New Hampshire Ave, NW
Washington, DC 20037
www.oxidayfoundation.org